Last call for an anonymous rendezvous with death . . .

There was little affection to be found in the company Evelyn now kept. But she tried to get her clients to spend the night. She was scared to sleep alone. The barman's shout of "Last call!" derailed her thoughts. She finished her drink and stepped outside in search of business. Some of the other girls were there, including Marjorie and Big Violet. She joined them for a cigarette.

A couple of Canadian soldiers hovered nearby, checking out the selection. One of them gave Evelyn a salacious look of approval. She liked the way he looked. He was handsome with an accent that hinted at weekends in the country and afternoon drives in the Rolls. He had a slim but powerful build. His smile dazzled, even in the darkness. Although he was younger than Evelyn preferred, she found him charming.

When she inquired as to his likes, he responded: "I like blondes. . . ."

"There was no inkling of the orgy of murder that was to follow."

—**Chief Superintendent Frederick Cherrill,
Head of Scotland Yard's Fingerprint Division**

Books by Simon Read

ON THE HOUSE
IN THE DARK

IN THE DARK

THE **TRUE STORY**
OF THE **BLACKOUT RIPPER**

SIMON READ

BERKLEY BOOKS, NEW YORK

THE BERKLEY PUBLISHING GROUP
Published by the Penguin Group
Penguin Group (USA) Inc.
375 Hudson Street, New York, New York 10014, USA
Penguin Group (Canada), 90 Eglinton Avenue East, Suite 700, Toronto, Ontario M4P 2Y3, Canada
(a division of Pearson Penguin Canada Inc.)
Penguin Books Ltd., 80 Strand, London WC2R 0RL, England
Penguin Group Ireland, 25 St. Stephen's Green, Dublin 2, Ireland (a division of Penguin Books Ltd.)
Penguin Group (Australia), 250 Camberwell Road, Camberwell, Victoria 3124, Australia
(a division of Pearson Australia Group Pty. Ltd.)
Penguin Books India Pvt. Ltd., 11 Community Centre, Panchsheel Park, New Delhi—110 017, India
Penguin Group (NZ), Cnr. Airborne and Rosedale Roads, Albany, Auckland 1310, New Zealand
(a division of Pearson New Zealand Ltd.)
Penguin Books (South Africa) (Pty.) Ltd., 24 Sturdee Avenue, Rosebank, Johannesburg 2196,
South Africa

Penguin Books Ltd., Registered Offices: 80 Strand, London WC2R 0RL, England

IN THE DARK

A Berkley Book / published by arrangement with the author

PRINTING HISTORY
Berkley mass-market edition / November 2006

Copyright © 2006 by Simon Read
Cover design by Steven Ferlauto
Cover photos: Knife: Orion / Dahlmann / Zefal / Corbis; London: Bettman / Corbis
Book design by Kristin del Rosario

ISBN: 0-425-21283-1

BERKLEY®
Berkley Books are published by The Berkley Publishing Group,
a division of Penguin Group (USA) Inc.,
375 Hudson Street, New York, New York 10014.
BERKLEY is a registered trademark of Penguin Group (USA) Inc.
The "B" design is a trademark belonging to Penguin Group (USA) Inc.

PRINTED IN THE UNITED STATES OF AMERICA

10 9 8 7 6 5 4 3 2 1

To Katie,
For all the wonderful reasons
. . . and not because you remind me of serial killers.

ACKNOWLEDGMENTS

This is my third book, yet repetition does not make the task of putting words on paper any easier. It's often said that no one writes a book alone, and it's very true—so many thanks to all the usual suspects for your friendship and support. Special mention goes to Danny Hoffman, Simon and Jessica Blint, Brian Reiser, and Ryan Sawyer. In England, much love and thanks to my family. My parents, Bill and Susan, have always been amazingly supportive. For this book, I drafted my father as a research assistant. Over Christmas 2004, he accompanied me to the British Public Records Office in Kew, London, and helped me wade through mountains of official documents. Research aside, he's always fun to grab a few pints with. A big thank-you goes out to my sister, Sarah, because she's become quite the cheerleader. Naturally, I have to thank Steve and his wife, Chris, who own and operate the Fish and Anchor pub in Evesham. If you ever get the chance, swing by for a visit. The food is great, the beer is strong, and the scotch is smooth. In the States, my agent, Ed Knappman, is always worthy of a hearty thank-you. Thanks to Samantha Mandor, my editor at Berkley, for her great assistance. If you ever visit Pleasanton, California, swing by Towne Centre Books on Main Street. Owner Judy Wheeler was wonderful helping spread the word about my first book, *On the House: The Bizarre Killing of Michael Malloy*. In that same regard, I want to thank Jim Ott and Kathy Cordova for having me on their show . . . twice. And, of course, there's Katie, who endured with amazing patience my endless fretting and fussing over the manuscript. She's fantastic.

Mike Brooks, a wonderful person, passed away while this book was in the editing phase. I feel very lucky to have had him as a close friend. He'll always be missed.

Not since the panic-ridden days in 1888, when Jack the Ripper was abroad in the East End, had London known such a reign of terror as that which existed in this wartime February, when, night after night, death—fiendish, revolting and gruesome—came to four unsuspecting women in the heart of the metropolis.

—Scotland Yard Chief Superintendent
Fred Cherrill

CONTENTS

FEBRUARY 9, 1942

ONE

A dark, cramped space of stagnant air, the bomb shelter's interior smelled of cold mortar and stale sweat. A stone seat ran the length of one inner wall, while, on the floor, an electric lantern cast a pallid circle of light across the morbid discovery made earlier that morning. The brick-built shelter was one of several on Montague Place, Marylebone—near Regent's Park in Central London—and one of countless similar structures that lined the streets of the capital. It was just shy of nine o'clock, and a harsh winter's sun backlit the city's shattered skyline. Daybreak came hard to London, a metropolis whose landscape had forever been altered by incendiary and high-explosive—but the air-raid sirens had remained silent the night before. The shelter that was the focus of attention was the center one in a grouping of three. Divisional Detective Inspector Leonard Clare of Albany Street Police Station, "D" Division, squinted against the cold. He knelt and stared into the shelter's entrance. An electrician, one Harold Batchelor, had found the body at 8:40 a.m. as he walked to work. Batchelor's calls for help had summoned Police Constable John Miles at 8:51 a.m. Senior officers were on the scene within four minutes. Batchelor gave his statement to a trench-coated detective. Clare straightened himself and stepped closer to hear what the man said.

"I was with my mate and I was walking through Dorset Street, across into Montague Street, and along Montague on the left-hand side going to Edgware Road," Batchelor said. "In between two of the shelters I saw the top of an electric torch. My mate went toward it and showed me something inside the shelter. I saw the body of a woman lying on her back."

Clare returned his attention to the shelter and the dead woman within. She lay on her back in the gutter, which cut through the shelter's center. Her feet pointed toward Gloucester Place, her right leg slightly raised and resting on an outcropping of brick in one corner of the shelter. She wore a fawn camel-hair coat and a green jumper. The right pocket of her overcoat held a sixpence. Her left leg was lying on the ground with her foot in the entrance. Her head was turned to the left, and her scarf was lying loosely over her face. Her skirt had been hiked up to her thighs. In the dim light, Clare could see the pale skin of the woman's exposed right breast where her white undershirt had been ripped away. Her underwear was stained with blood, as was the top of one stocking. Her gloves had been placed on top of her body, palms facing upward with the fingers pointing toward her face. Her tongue protruded between her teeth, slightly swollen. Lying near the body were a box of Master's safety matches and a tin of Ovaltine tablets. Her wristwatch had stopped at one o'clock, but started ticking again when Clare removed it from her wrist. A green woolen cap lay across the shelter's threshold. Clare ordered that loose scrapings of mortar both inside and outside the shelter's entrance be collected as evidence. Sergeant Percy Law from the Photograph Branch took pictures of the crime scene.

At 9:10 a.m., Dr. Alexander Baldie—the divisional police surgeon—arrived at the shelter. A police constable turned on a crime-scene lamp at the shelter's entrance, burning away the shadows that clung to the brick interior, allowing Baldie to begin his examination. He observed two superficial pressure abrasions across the neck where some skin had apparently been rubbed off. The skin below the left side of her chin showed bruising, with heavy discoloration around her Adam's apple. Her extremities and head were cold, but the parts of her body still covered by clothing were slightly warm. Rigor mortis was in partial onset, indicating the woman had been dead for no more than several hours.

"The appearances here are consistent with death by manual strangulation," Baldie said to Clare as he climbed out of the shelter. "You'll obviously know more following the autopsy."

Clare nodded and turned his head as someone approached from behind.

"Morning, Inspector."

The voice was that of Detective Chief Superintendent Frederick Cherrill, head of Scotland Yard's Fingerprint Department. For more than two decades he had applied his special trade with vigor, searching for murderers in bloody swirls left on knife handles and straight-edged razors; looking for the identities of killers in powdered smudges lifted from furniture and panes of glass. The thrill of such discoveries never lost its appeal to Cherrill who, despite his senior rank, insisted on working murder scenes himself. He was

Oxford born and bred, and looked the part in his bowler hat. Wisps of silver hair protruded from under the brim, and in situations like this he thrived. Now Clare stepped aside and allowed Cherrill to enter the shelter to conduct his own examination. Crouched on his haunches, the fingerprint man gave the body a cursory glance. It seemed to him the woman had been hurriedly dumped in the shelter after being strangled in the street. Like the police surgeon, Cherrill's attention focused on the dark bruising of the woman's neck. From inside his jacket pocket, he withdrew his magnifying glass and bent low over the woman's throat. He slowly passed the magnifying glass—which he carried with him at all times—over the bruises in a back-and-forth motion.

"Anything?" Clare asked from outside the shelter.

Lost in thought, Cherrill didn't answer immediately. He hoped to find some marking on the neck or a deformity to the bruises that might suggest an irregularity in the fingers of the killer. He found nothing. Still looking intently through his magnifying glass, Cherrill told Clare, "The man who did this is left handed." The bruises indicated as much. The left side of the neck sported one deep purplish bruise, while the opposite side displayed a cluster of discoloration where the remaining four digits had sunk into the flesh, thus indicating the deadly grasp of a left-handed individual. Casting his gaze down the body, he noticed some scratches on the heel of her shoes indicative of a struggle. But aside from the bruising, nothing on the corpse provided Cherrill with any clues. Perhaps some of the woman's possessions now strewn about would yield more helpful information. He ordered a constable to make sure they reached him for analysis that afternoon at the Yard.

Cherrill crawled out of the shelter and straightened himself in the early morning cold. A light snow had fallen the night before and was now turning to a thin slush beneath his feet. He had joined the Yard's Fingerprint Department in 1920 as a constable and rapidly worked his way up the ranks. He had seen death in all its various forms and experienced human nature at its lowest. The London Blitz had given rise to stirring tales of self-sacrifice and heroism— but it also exacerbated the worst of the city's criminal element. How many murders had he worked since the outbreak of hostilities? Too many—and yet, a certain irony could be found in each one. Take this dead woman for example. How many air raids had she survived? How many nights had she been dragged from the warmth of her bed by the wailing of sirens? She had lived through Hitler's bombs only to be robbed of life by something far more petty.

As Cherrill stood pondering the woman before him, detectives and uniformed constables spread out to knock on doors and question residents. They needed to establish a time of death and identify the victim. She was a slender woman with black hair and high cheekbones—a woman not wholly unattractive. From where Cherrill stood, he could just make out the brown skirt bunched around her thighs. Cherrill's silent reflection was broken by the approach of a constable who identified himself to Clare as Arthur Cyril Williams, a war reserve constable working out of the Marylebone Lane Police Station. Williams reported he had inspected the shelters the night before while walking his beat, but saw nothing unusual.

"I got on duty last night at ten," he said, while Clare scribbled in his notebook. "I'm posted to No. 13 beat, which covers Marylebone Road, Baker Street, York Street, Montague Place and Seymour Place."

Williams said he passed by the bomb shelter at 11:20 p.m.

"I usually look inside these shelters when I pass—and

I did last night. I shined my light up and down, but didn't see anyone in the shelters at all. I think if anyone had been lying on the floor, I would have noticed them. I did not hear anything unusual. It was a very quiet night with very few people about and no moon. It was very dark."

Come nightfall, London sank into a black oblivion. Residents extinguished all light to thwart enemy bombers, at the expense of wreaking some havoc on the ground. The first campaign waged by British women on the home front was one against illumination, stitching countless thousands of yards of dark-colored material into blackout curtains. The dark blue, dark green and black drapes were now ritually drawn across all the windows in the capital by sunset. Light could not be permitted to escape any building. The curtains could not be washed, as this made them more permeable to light. Instead, the government dispensed booklets instructing people to vacuum, shake, brush and iron their curtains to make them more effective. The drill instructor–like shriek of "Put out that light!" became a common sound on the nighttime streets of London, as air-raid precaution wardens roamed neighborhoods in search of blackout violations. It had been that way since the blackout went into effect on August 31, 1939—three days before the morbid voice of Prime Minister Neville Chamberlain came over the BBC and told an anxious nation it again braved war with Germany. In the business of keeping things dark, public transit received little leeway. Bus and taxi operators had to cover their headlights in a fashion that allowed only the most minimal amount of light to escape. The result was a lot of distraught drivers standing over the writhing—and sometimes still—figures of the pedestrians they had hit in the middle of the street. Nocturnal London had become an alien world of rumbling shadows and fleeting figures.

"What people there were about were soldiers," Williams told Clare. "Four or five times during the night I was asked where the Church Army Hostel was." Williams waved an arm in some general direction: "It's in Seymour Place, and I directed the person making inquiries on each occasion."

Williams said that just before midnight he was ordered to Baker Street to monitor some shady figures reportedly seen moving in and out of a doorway at No. 114. The surveillance yielded nothing of consequence, and Williams took lunch from 1:15 a.m. to 2:15 a.m.

"I passed by the shelters while patrolling the other side of the street two or three more times during the night," he said. "I didn't hear anything unusual as far as I can remember. There were no vehicles in the street when I passed, and I didn't see a sentry on duty."

Clare closed his notebook, thanked the constable and sent him on his way. The London underworld had made an overt move aboveground, for the blackout provided ideal cover for those who fancied lawless pursuits. It was hard to identify someone passing on the street in black silhouette. Most attention these nights was directed skyward. Firewatchers on the lookout for German incendiaries manned the roofs of factories and other businesses. Fires provided a homing beacon for the Luftwaffe. Blazes, once ignited, had to be put out as soon as possible. ARP wardens hit the streets armed with stirrup pumps ready to battle the slightest spark. Some criminals saw an ideal opportunity in being ARPs. It gave them easy access to bombed homes and office buildings, and the possessions within. Clare shook his head and looked at his watch. It showed 10:15 a.m. as Police Constable Miles— the first officer on the scene—approached. He held something in his gloved hand, a woman's black handbag, wet, torn and empty. Miles said it had been discovered lying on the pavement on Wyndham Street, not far removed from the murder scene. Whether prints could be lifted from it was questionable, but it was bagged with the dead woman's other possessions. Once back at the Yard, Cherrill would dust everything and compare the prints he lifted with those already on file with the Metropolitan Police Department.

Other than the woman's few scant possessions, the crime scene had yielded no useful information—no bloody fingerprints and no identifiable footprints. Now, as the mortuary wagon approached, Clare hoped the door-to-door questioning would offer some hint as to the previous night's events. At 10:30 a.m., mortician workers removed the body from the shelter, loaded it onto a stretcher and placed it in the back of the wagon. It was promptly taken to the Paddington Mortuary, where the pathologist's blade awaited.

Sir Edward Henry, the future police commissioner, established Scotland Yard's Fingerprint Department in 1901. The following year, Harry Jackson—a small-time burglar—became the first person jailed for a crime based on fingerprint evidence. A jury heard the case at the Old Bailey—London's Central Criminal Court—on September 13, 1902, after Jackson pleaded not guilty to stealing billiard balls from a home in South London. At the crime scene, Jackson left an imprint of his left thumb on a newly painted windowsill. The print had been discovered and photographed by one Detective Sergeant Collins, who searched the Yard's then-small collection of fingerprints taken from known criminals. A match surfaced based on a visual comparison of the print's looping pattern to those prints in the index. Police quickly nabbed Jackson—a forty-one-year-old laborer—who, upon being convicted, received a seven-year prison sentence.

Three years later, on March 27, 1905, Mr. and Mrs. Farrow were attacked and killed in their shop on Deptford High Street in a crime dubbed "The Mask Murders," so named because the killers left masks made of black stockings behind at the scene. Investigators who searched the shop found an empty cashbox with a thumbprint inside. Detectives at the Fingerprint Department inspected the box. They photographed the print and set about the laborious task of going through the Yard's ever-increasing print index, which now boasted eighty thousand sets of finger impressions. Their search, however, proved futile—but a break in the case soon evolved when police, acting on statements from witnesses, arrested two brothers named Albert and Alfred Stratton. Once in custody, their prints were taken and compared to the one found on the cashbox. It was a match with Alfred's right thumb. The brothers' fates were decided. After being convicted of murder at the Old Bailey, the two were sent to the gallows.

Cherrill's work with the Fingerprint Department had made him something of a celebrity with other lawmen and the media of the day. A favorite subject of newspaper photographers, he would purposely situate himself at crime scenes in a location where he could be easily photographed without giving the impression he was posing for the shot. Cherrill read fingerprints with the same casual ease and interest that most people read the morning paper over breakfast. In one instance, he identified a killer based on fingerprint evidence within hours of arriving at a crime scene. The case itself proved unexceptional, but the speed at which it was solved distinguished it from others.

Theodora Greenhill had been killed in the drawing room of her Kensington flat the year before. One of Greenhill's daughters discovered the body stretched across the floor with a handkerchief placed over the face and a ligature tied around the neck. The daughter had become suspicious and let herself in when no one answered a knock on the flat's door. Upon responding, Detective Chief Inspector William Salisbury quickly deduced that Greenhill had been attacked while penning a letter at her writing desk. He found a piece of paper with the beginnings of a note: "Received from Dr. H. D. Trevor the s . . ." The "s" trailed off the page in a messy line where Greenhill had dragged the pen across the paper as she fell to the floor. Once down and incapacitated from a blow to the head with a beer bottle, she had been choked to death. Although the room showed no signs of a struggle, someone had rummaged through the drawers of Greenhill's desk.

The fact a beer bottle had been used in the assault was easy to ascertain as pieces of broken glass littered the floor and were found in a wastebasket in the flat. Salisbury called for Cherrill and awaited his arrival. When Cherrill arrived with magnifying glass in hand and customary bowler hat on his head, he wasted no time hunting for prints. His expedition through the crime scene proved fruitful, producing a bloody thumbprint on a table near the body and a print under the table. He also collected nearly one hundred pieces of glass from the shattered bottle and found prints on four of them. In Greenhill's bedroom, he found a print on a moneybox that had been pried open and emptied of its contents. Cherrill returned to the drawing room and saw the note with the name "Trevor" on it. Something inside him clicked. He placed a call to the Criminal Records Office and asked that the files on all men using the name Trevor be delivered to Greenhill's flat.

Salisbury raised a skeptical eyebrow as Cherrill took a seat and waited for the documents to be delivered. When they finally arrived in a thick stack, Cherrill brought his magnifying glass up to his eye and began a methodical comparison between the prints in the files and those found on the pieces of glass, the table and the moneybox. It was not long before Cherrill identified the man Salisbury wanted: Harold Dorian Trevor. At the time of this announcement, the body of Mrs. Greenhill still lay unceremoniously between the two men. Salisbury and his men, acting on Cherrill's advice, tracked Trevor in less than twenty-four hours and arrested him in Wales. With his penchant for wearing a monocle—and aliases such as Lord Reginald Herbert—Trevor was a colorful character whose desire to live a life of luxury without actually working had propelled him to take violent action.

The sixty-two-year-old had visited Mrs. Greenhill to discuss renting her flat. He wrote her a check then slammed a bottle against her head when she sat down to write a receipt. As she lay on the floor dazed and moaning, he choked the life out of her. After being found guilty of murder, he met with the hangman at Wandsworth Prison.

But cases of such simplicity were the exception, not the rule. The case of the woman in the air-raid shelter did not surrender its secrets so quickly. Following the removal of the body, Cherrill promptly returned to the Yard to analyze the items taken from the scene.

The lifting of fingerprints is a delicate task, requiring a gentle touch and a steady hand. In his office, Cherrill dabbed a feather brush into a jar of white powder. Just as each stroke of an artist's brush creates an image where before there was nothing but a blank canvas, so too did Cherrill's brush on the battered surface of the woman's bag. He moved his wrist with rhythmic grace and guided the brush with his fingers. The chemical composition of fingerprint powders can vary, but they all basically work the same way. Latent fingerprints are created by the natural secretion of sweat and oils from the skin that leave behind an outline of the friction ridges found on one's fingers. A person's fingerprints remain constant from the womb to the grave. Only damage to the skin of the finger can cause alterations to the print. Each print is wholly unique to an individual—even the prints of identical twins differ. When fingerprint powder makes contact with the swirling patterns of grease and oil left by someone's touch, the powder particles adhere to the secretions and render the print visible to the human eye.

Faint white swirls began to take shape like forms materializing in a fog as the powder settled on the bag's black surface. But even as the prints appeared, Cherrill knew a positive latent match did not guarantee a conviction. The murder of one Walter Dinivan in 1936 had established that sour point, and the case remained a source of frustration for Cherrill. Dinivan, a wealthy retiree, had been found murdered in his granddaughter's home in Bournemouth. Such force had been used to bash the man's head in that pieces of his skull were found embedded in his brain. His face revealed a bloody and shattered mess, and marks on his neck suggested someone had tried to strangle him.

There were no signs of struggle in the room where Dinivan had died, but a beer glass rested on its side on a nearby table. The glass was sent to Cherrill, who was able to lift a thumbprint from it. In the meantime, the investigation—headed by the Yard's Detective Chief Inspector Burt—moved forward. Found at the scene and removed as evidence were a woman's curling iron and a paper bag. Inquiries in town soon revealed that a man named Joseph Williams had been seen flashing a lot of cash the day after the murder. Witnesses found such behavior unusual because

Williams—a one-time soldier who served in India and fought for the Empire—had been poverty-stricken. When Burt paid a visit to Williams's house, he found the man living in disgusting squalor. Truculent by nature, Williams told the Yard man, when Burt attempted to question him, to go to hell.

When police checked with Williams a short time later, he agreed to let them look around his house. During the search, Burt's partner found a pile of paper bags—similar to the one found at the crime scene—and removed several as evidence. Burt, meanwhile, asked Williams if he could take a look at his wallet. Williams said yes. It was stuffed near-to-bursting with paper money, the result, Williams said, of a fortunate pick at the local racetrack. Burt promptly confiscated the cash, despite Williams's violent protests. The detectives left and took the evidence back to the Yard. An examination of the bags under ultraviolet light showed them to have a texture identical to the one found at the crime scene. Detectives traced the money taken from Williams to the bank where Dinivan cashed his retirement checks each week. The odd piece of the puzzle was the woman's curling iron found near the body. Burt believed it had been placed at the scene to fool police into thinking the killer was female.

Burt's hunch was born out. Detectives tracked down Williams's ex-wife, who told them that when she lived with Williams years before she used a curling iron just like the one found at Dinivan's place. Convinced he had a suspect, Burt returned to Williams's squalid home to confront him with the evidence. Williams insisted he was innocent. Burt asked Williams to prove it by letting police take his fingerprints. Williams acquiesced, and the prints were immediately rushed to Cherrill for examination. It took less than an hour for Cherrill to match one of the prints to that found on the glass recovered at the crime scene. Investigators promptly arrested Williams, and the case went to trial.

In October 1939, despite all the evidence presented by the prosecution—including Cherrill's testimony regarding the fingerprint match—a jury found Williams not guilty. The verdict staggered Scotland Yard and was partly attributed to the defendant's incessant cries of innocence during the trial, which was heavily covered by the media. (Following Williams's death in 1951, the *News of the World* ran a story in which it revealed that Williams—on the night of his acquittal—admitted to a reporter he had killed Dinivan.) The thought of it now rankled Cherrill, whose motto had always been "Fingerprints never lie." He studied the bag's surface. He could now see the directional flow of the loops and swirls, and he guided his brush accordingly. Satisfied with his handiwork, he put the brush aside and picked up a camera. He selected a well-defined print and snapped a picture. With a piece of lifting tape, he removed excess powder from the print, being careful not to allow air bubbles to form beneath the tape. He held one end of the tape down with his left hand and rolled it flat over the print with his right, then carefully pulled it away. He applied the tape to a black background, allowing the white print to stand out in contrast. He repeated the process with several other prints.

A set of prints taken from the victim at the mortuary sat on the table in front of him. As rigor mortis had only started to set in, it had not been that difficult a task. Lifting prints from a person as stiff as a board required investigators to straighten the fingers. More often than not, this could be done by pressing down on the middle knuckle. With the woman, however, it had not been necessary—Cherrill simply dusted each finger with black powder and obtained the prints with lifting tape. He stuck each print to a white index card and marked each finger accordingly, then compared the prints on the bag to the prints taken from the victim.

To the casual observer, fingerprints are complex maps that may or may not lead to an identification. To Cherrill, however, they were familiar landscapes that could get you where you wanted to go if you knew how to read them. There were arches and tented arches, ulnar and radial loops, and whorls. He closed his mind to everything but the dizzying patterns framed within his magnifying glass, which he passed back and forth over the prints taken from the body and those lifted from the bag. He took notes and mapped each intricate pattern. It didn't take long for Cherrill to realize—much to his dismay—that the prints lifted from the bag were those of the deceased. He lifted prints from the other objects found in the shelter. The results were all the same. This, of course, was not entirely a surprise. The cold temperature the previous night meant the killer had probably worn gloves.

Cherrill set his magnifying glass down on the table. He'd had no reason to suspect the case would be easy, for nothing in wartime London proved simple.

A piece of dead flesh—measuring seven inches by six inches—had secured Sir Bernard Spilsbury's reputation. To the British public, his name was synonymous with the morbid, and it all began in 1910 with the tantalizing case of Dr. Crippen, an extraordinary affair for its day, complete with a transatlantic chase and Scotland Yard's first usage of wireless communications.

On July 13 of that year, police summoned Spilsbury, then a young doctor at St. Mary's Hospital, Paddington, to a house at 39 Hilldrop Crescent in Camden Town near Regent's Park. There, Scotland Yard Chief Inspector Walter Dew escorted him into the basement, where a headless body had been found buried in lime. It was impossible to identify the body's sex. The remains had been wrapped in a pair of men's pajamas, and the organs in the chest and stomach had been removed. The arms and legs also had been severed and discarded. Traces of hyocin—a highly lethal toxin—were found in the body. Dew told Spilsbury that he believed the body was that of Mrs. Cora Crippen, the wife of an American doctor living in London. Dew said Mrs. Crippen's friends had reported her missing a few weeks prior and told police they suspected her husband, Dr. Peter Hawley Harvey Crippen, of foul play. They told detectives that Dr. Crippen had been seen some weeks earlier at a cocktail party with his typist, Ms. Ethel LeNeve, at his side. When friends asked about his wife, Crippen said she had recently died while on a trip to California and had been cremated stateside. The fact LeNeve wore one of Cora Crippen's expensive brooches cast the story in a dubious light.

Dew had interviewed Crippen at the Hilldrop Crescent house a few days after his wife had been reported missing. The doctor told Dew his wife was really alive and living in Chicago with her new lover. He said he was ashamed of his wife's tawdry behavior and had fabricated the story of her death to spare his pride. Dew—who, as a young constable, had been the first officer to respond to the scene of Jack the Ripper's fifth and final victim—doubted the doctor's story. When Dew returned a few days later on July 13 to interview the doctor a second time, he found that Crippen had fled. A search of the house quickly yielded the body in the basement. Dew had promptly contacted St. Mary's Hospital for an available pathologist to come and examine the remains. On July 16, an arrest warrant for Crippen and LeNeve was issued. The papers went wild with the story and splashed it across their front pages. The media frenzy only intensified when officials learned on July 22 that Crippen and his lover had fled across the Atlantic on a steamship bound for Canada.

Scotland Yard sent a wireless communiqué to all ships sailing to foreign ports, urging captains and their crews to watch for the two fugitives. The captain of the SS *Montrose* had received the wire and promptly responded. On July 14, two passengers—a Mr. Johnson and his sixteen-year-old son—had boarded the *Montrose* in Antwerp. The captain immediately noted that something about the two seemed strange. Although supposedly father and son, they walked the decks hand in hand. The boy spoke with a very high voice and always crossed his legs when he sat down. Scotland Yard received the following wireless message from the *Montrose*'s captain on July 22: "Have strong suspicion that Crippen London Cellar murderer and accomplice are amongst saloon passengers. Moustache shaved off, growing a beard. Accomplice dressed as a boy, voice, manner undoubtedly a girl."

Dew immediately booked passage on a faster ship, raced across the Atlantic and beat Crippen to Montreal by two days. The doctor and his lover were arrested when their ship reached port, promptly shipped back to England and stood trial at the Central Criminal Court for "the murder and mutilation" of Cora Crippen. The trial helped push Spilsbury's name into the national consciousness. Oxford educated, the thirty-three-year-old Spilsbury, a man of little humor and grim disposition, offered testimony crucial to the prosecution's case. Spilsbury had positively identified the remains found in Crippen's basement as Cora

Crippen. That piece of skin—the one measuring seven inches by six inches—made the identification possible. The skin, removed from the lower-front abdomen, had a scar on it. Cora Crippen's sister testified that her sister had a scar on her lower-front abdomen, the result of an operation she'd had to remove her ovaries. The defense argued that the scar was merely a fold in the skin brought on by death. But with microscope, slides and a long explanation on the properties of scars, Spilsbury disproved the defense's theory. The jury listened and convicted Crippen of murder after deliberating for a mere half hour. Authorities released LeNeve from custody after she had been found not guilty of being an accessory after the fact. On November 28, 1910, less than one mile from where he buried his wife, Crippen had his date with the hangman.

Over the next three decades—through his graphic testimony and medical expertise—Spilsbury would be instrumental in sending hundreds of murderers to the gallows. He performed thousands of autopsies, including those of the men his testimony condemned to death. In short order, his name became associated with Britain's most notorious crimes—cases so violent and bizarre, they rivaled the most outrageous works of detective fiction.

At 2:30 p.m. on February 9, Spilsbury took his scalpel to the woman's body found in the air-raid shelter. The corpse lay on a metal gurney with a circular hole drilled between the ankles to drain the blood. Detective Inspector Clare looked on. Externally, she appeared to be a well-nourished woman who, in life, stood about five feet, four inches tall. The postmortem stains on her skin were livid, as were her lips and fingernails. Her pupils were dilated and the whites of her eyes were clouded with blood and marred with hemorrhages. Spilsbury noted tiny hemorrhages in the skin of her forehead and behind the eyelids. Above her left eyebrow, a superficial abrasion ran about one-half inch in length. Starting at the point of her chin and running along her right jawline was a bruise more than two inches long. Three inches below the jaw were two linear abrasions across the front of the neck. Both abrasions measured about an inch in length and were three-eighths of an inch apart. Two faint abrasions—one of them curved in the shape of a fingernail—scarred the neck about an inch above the two linear marks. There was an abrasion on the right of the neck and an abrasion on the back of the neck, level with the wounds in the front.

The lower part of the victim's right breast was bloodied by a number of small abrasions and a scratch etched into the skin nearly two inches long. Her legs were bruised. Spilsbury photographed the woman's face, then, taking scalpel in hand, he cut her open. The deep surface of her scalp had numerous hemorrhages, and a bruise was evident just above the right temple. Her organs were congested with blood and there were more hemorrhages on the surface of her heart. Her airways were clogged with blood and froth. The force of the grip at her throat was evident in the cricoid cartilage of the larynx, which had been fractured on both sides, with bleeding around the fractures. There were additional hemorrhages in the muscles of the neck and a bruise below the angle of the left jaw. Both sides of the victim's tongue were bruised heavily.

"The tonsils," Spilsbury noted, "were engorged with blood."

A large amount of food—some of which appeared to be beetroot—in an advanced stage of digestion remained in the woman's stomach. Aside from some blood in her vagina, her genitals appeared to be uninjured. Spilsbury put down his scalpel and turned to Clare. "The cause of death was as-phyxia due to strangulation by the hand, based on the abrasions and bruises on the front of her neck," he said. "The distribution of the injuries on the neck suggests they were inflicted by the left hand. There was no spermatozoa in the vagina." Nor was there a motive for the killing or a clue as to the woman's identity.

Technicians developed the picture Spilsbury took later that afternoon. The black-and-white image did nothing to soften the grisly nature of the woman's condition. Clare ordered that copies of it be made and distributed to show residents in the neighborhood where the body had been discovered.

Somebody had to know something.

TWO

Ivy Cecilia Poole, forty-nine, worked as a fun-fair attendant and couldn't help but notice the near-constant flow of men that passed through her neighbor's adjoining apartment at 153 Wardour Street. Perhaps the foot traffic was not too surprising, for her neighbor—Evelyn Oatley, sometimes called Leta Ward—was quite the looker: blond, with a slim waist and full breasts. But it wasn't that Mrs. Poole made such things her business. Proximity all but guaranteed that privacy was virtually nonexistent. The two living quarters had originally been one large room, but were rendered separate by a dividing wall that consisted of nothing more than two folding doors. One woman couldn't help but be aware of what the other was doing.

Evelyn, thirty-four, the wife of a one-time poultry farmer in Blackpool, had come to the city in 1936 to pursue a career on the London stage, but the outbreak of war thwarted her ambitions. Theater tickets were no longer in great demand, and acting jobs were few and far between. To make ends meet, she worked as a hostess in various nightclubs. She worked the streets during her off hours to make a little extra, trolling the blackout for men in need of temporary company and fleeting affection. These were the men Ivy Poole saw coming and going with unceasing regularity. Evelyn's estranged husband apparently knew of his wife's behavior, but tried not to make an issue of it. After all, they had been living apart for the past six years, and she had to make a living somehow. He made a point of venturing to the capital to visit his wife when he could. In 1941, he visited twice and stayed for a week on both occasions. Most recently, he had stayed with her from January 26 to February 3, during which time Evelyn introduced him to Ivy.

But within hours of escorting her husband to the Euston Train Station and waving him back to Blackpool, Evelyn had returned to entertaining men in her cramped apartment. Many people would frown upon such behavior, but not Ivy—she was a sympathetic neighbor and blessed with patience. It was just as well, as from February 3 to the night of Saturday, February 7, Evelyn had a man in her room every evening after 11 p.m. She did her best to obscure the carnal noises emanating from her side of the dividing wall by playing her wireless. It was certainly better than listening to the alternative.

On Sunday, February 8, Evelyn emerged from her apartment shortly after 1 p.m. and visited with Ivy. She had a piece of steak with her and asked if she could cook it on Ivy's stovetop. Such a delicacy was rare, and the two women dined together, passing the time with idle conversation. Evelyn volunteered to clean the dishes after dinner, and Ivy went to work at the fun fair in Leicester Square. When Ivy returned home at 10 p.m., she found Evelyn's door open and went in to say hello.

"My, you're home early tonight," she said when she saw Evelyn sitting on her bed with a towel wrapped around her head.

"I just wanted to wash my hair," Evelyn said. "Besides, I never go anywhere on Sundays. I'm just going to go to bed."

Ivy left Evelyn, returned to her own space, and retired for the evening.

While police canvassed Montague Place on Monday, February 9, Evelyn Oatley entertained a lady friend. The sound of conversation drifted through Evelyn's open door into Ivy's place.

"Oh, Ivy," Evelyn called, "do bring your cat over here and show my friend."

Ivy put down her newspaper and scooped the fat tabby off the small dining table. She carried the purring creature next door, where Evelyn sat chatting with her companion. The guest was a strange-looking woman in her early thirties with a dark complexion. Except for a large red hat, the woman wore all black. She took little notice of the cat, but the fuss and attention Evelyn gave the animal more than compensated for her friend's lack of interest. Neither Ivy nor the strange woman said anything to each other.

Ivy went back to her apartment, placed her cat on the table and resumed reading the newspaper, oblivious to the fact that she and Evelyn had just shared their last meaningful exchange.

*   *   *

He lusted for a blonde, and in Soho he knew he would find one. A hectic architectural cluster of both chic and seedy, Soho had long been his favorite haunt. Sex and drink could be had in vast quantities, and he readily availed himself of such pleasures. The area was a microcosm of London. Bordered by Oxford Street to the north, Piccadilly Circus and Leicester Square to the south, Charing Cross Road to the east and Regent Street to the west, Soho was—and remains—a multicultural extravaganza of rich and poor. Theaters and restaurants stood in close proximity to brothels and clubs of ill repute. Tuxedo-clad theatergoers shared street space with hookers and pimps, though the war had drastically reduced the demand for theater tickets. His interests, however, were more carnal than cultural. He enjoyed eyeing the wares of street-corner women and asking them what they had to offer. His tastes varied and fluctuated from one moment to the next. Although he craved a blonde this evening, tomorrow he might find himself hungering for a brunette.

Whatever his particular fancies, he never had trouble securing the affections of the opposite sex—whether he was paying for it or simply relying on his natural charm. Never one to exude warmth, he exercised an icy detachment in his casual encounters that leant him an air of danger and intrigue—characteristics some women seemed to like. Also accounting for his success with women were his above-average looks. He cut a dashing figure in his military uniform and employed an accent suggesting a background far more noble than his working-class roots. In the blackout, Piccadilly Circus was far removed from the dazzling nighttime spectacle it had once been. Its great neon signs hung lifeless off the sides of buildings, and the famed statue of Eros—the god of love and the son of Aphrodite—hid from view, and bombs, behind an ugly pyramid of cement slabs.

Buses lumbered cautiously by in the pitch black, and soldiers loitered near dark alleys waiting for some anonymous rendezvous. Such encounters were not hard to come by. Women working the streets hung around in doorways and alleys between pubs, shining their electric torches on their feet as potential customers casually ambled past. There was always a nearby room, a deserted spot in the alley or a surface air-raid shelter in which business could be conducted. On this particular evening, Monday, February 9, the man wearing the dress uniform of the British Royal Air Force didn't care where he was taken as long as the woman did what he expected of her. He was out for a night on the town, and he had brought a friend with him.

The two men found what they were looking for outside the Monico Restaurant. The time was nearly 11 p.m. and the pubs were preparing to close—but it hardly mattered, as both men had consumed plenty of drink in the hours before and were feeling somewhat unsteady on their feet. They had started their evening with two large whiskeys in the Princes Bar in Piccadilly, before moving onto the Monico Restaurant near Regent Street. There, the two airmen engaged a group of civilians in conversation, bought several rounds of whiskey and befriended an American serving in the RAF. The Yank was meeting a date at 7:30 p.m. at the Chandos Public House in Trafalgar Square and asked the two airmen to join him after they had finished their drinks. Shortly after the American's departure, the two airmen left the Monico for the Salted Almond Bar at the Trocadero. They stayed for twenty minutes and gulped down two highballs each before catching up with the American at the Chandos, where more whiskeys were consumed.

The Brits eventually left the Yank alone with his lady friend. Outside, they hailed a taxi and took it to Martinez's, the Spanish restaurant on Swallow Street. They consumed sherries in the lounge before moving into the cellar dining room, where they ate dinner and shared a bottle of wine. Sometime around 10:30 p.m. they emerged from the restaurant and made their way back to Piccadilly Circus. There, outside the Monico Restaurant, two women loitering near the doorway grabbed their attention. One of them was blond. The airman caught a faint glimpse of her hair when she flashed her torch on herself.

Her name was Laura Denmark, and she had been working the street with her friend Molly. The night had been quiet. Several Canadian soldiers had engaged the girls in pointless conversation before vanishing into the night. Laura didn't care for window shoppers. If a man liked the merchandise, he was expected to make a reasonable offer. After all, she wasn't out here for show. Laura was saying as much to Molly, when she saw the two airmen approaching. One of them was quite tall, about six feet, with a mustache and a head of unruly blond hair that protruded from beneath his cap, and what struck her as a classy accent. Via the glow of her torch, she could see his large mouth and impressive dental work. He boasted a medium build and looked to be in good shape. She guessed him to be somewhere in his mid-twenties.

"What's that?" she asked, pointing to a white slip sticking out of his cap.

"Oh, that shows that I'm training to be an officer and joined the RAF before the war," he said, speaking with a broad smile.

Laura nodded and turned her head slightly. His words came to her on breath soured by wine and whiskey.

"What's your name?" she asked.

"Gordon," he said. "That's Felix."

Felix was lost in conversation with Molly, a short, curvy

woman with a fat face. He, too, had a white slip stuck in his cap, and seemed to be on the verge of working out a deal with his lady companion. She told him for a pound he could get it all. Felix considered the offer only for the briefest of moments before deciding it was satisfactory. He nodded his approval.

"I have a room just over there," Molly told Felix, waving her arm in the general direction of the Regent Palace. "When we're done, I'll bring you back here—but you might have to wait for your friend. Laura lives a bit further away."

"That's not a problem," said Felix, shooting an eager smile Gordon's way.

Laura watched her friend and Felix wander off. "Well, Gordon," she said, "what's your fancy?"

"Blondes."

The two walked side by side, their way guided by the thin beam of light cast by Laura's torch. Their breath hung heavy and white in the frigid darkness, and the sky glowed blue and white as long fingers of light probed the black expanse. They made their way toward Shaftesbury Avenue and eventually turned onto Frith Street, where Laura kept a room at No. 47. The room was a cramped and squalid affair with a single bed in one corner and an electric fire in the other. In the dim light of the room, Laura asked her date for the pre-agreed-upon pound. The airman reached into his pocket and pulled out a bill.

"If you give me another, you can stay longer," Laura said.

The airman slipped her an additional thirty shillings.

With the business aspect taken care of, Laura told the man to take off his clothes. As he did so, she noticed his moves were mildly unsteady and that he was wobbly with drink. He stripped down to his undershirt, underpants and socks. Laura removed her dress and presented herself to him in stockings and a slip. They moved to the bed and lay down side by side. His hands moved slowly across her body, venturing beneath her slip before running down the smooth surface of her stockings. She could feel the blood in him stir and reached for the nightstand to grab a "preventative." She pulled down his pants and rolled the condom on, then—in a tone that was neither seductive nor beckoning—told him to get on top. The bed creaked as he moved his body into position. He slipped himself into her and mindlessly banged away. There was nothing passionate about it, and the closeness of their bodies was completely devoid of eroticism.

Laura lay there with her eyes closed and gave the obligatory groan with each awkward thrust of the airman's hips. His breath came and went in heavy rasps, and was warm on her face. She could still smell the drink in him. Sometimes they were quick to finish the job—other times they took an eternity. With each man she went through the motions with little enthusiasm, feigning minimal sexual interest. The repetitive nature of the job had numbed the risqué excitement of it countless clients ago. For ten minutes she lay there, breathing in his musk and the scent of cheap wine and whiskey. He was thrusting harder, but she could feel him going soft. The more he diminished inside her, the harder he pushed. But he was soon overcome by the sudden misfortune of biology and rolled off her. He collapsed on the sheets beside her out of breath and unfulfilled.

Laura said nothing, but she could feel his skin against hers slick with perspiration. Some men would respond to such an embarrassing situation with a violent outburst, but the airman simply chuckled and patted Laura on the thigh.

"I think I've had too much to drink," he said before mounting her a second time. She worked his crotch with her hand and got him hard again. He slipped himself inside her and thrust away for another fifteen minutes, only to be thwarted by a similar outcome.

"Get off me," Laura said, her patience expended.

The airman complied. She removed the condom with one hand and sat on the edge of the bed. Her skin glowed slightly red in the weak light of the electric fire as she dropped the prophylactic in a wastebasket.

"I'm sorry, Blondie," he said.

She shrugged nonchalantly and smiled. "Let's sit in front of the fire."

They sat together on the floor. He ran his right hand through her shoulder-length hair and began stroking himself with his left hand.

"I like your hair, Blondie," he said. "I like blondes."

She put another condom on him. The last thing she wanted to do was spend her evening scrubbing a mess out of the carpet. With his right hand still in her hair, he began jerking his left hand with increasing urgency. He took her hair in a fist and gently tugged on it, pulling her head slightly back, all the while exclaiming his love for blondes. Laura felt the grip on her hair tighten as he lifted his head toward the ceiling and closed his eyes. He ran his tongue over his lips, tasting his own sweat. As his left hand moved ever faster, his verbal admiration for her hair devolved into a series of loud moans. And then it was over. He released his grip on her hair and slumped forward as if suddenly relieved of some heavy burden. He buried his face in his hands and wiped the sweat from his eyes before peeling off the condom. Holding the filled rubber out at arm's length, he cast a quizzical glance in Laura's direction. She took it between forefinger and thumb and tossed it in the wastebasket with the other.

They remained sitting in front of the fire for several minutes. His head was swooning from the heat, the alcohol and the self-inflicted orgasm. He kept running a hand over his face and through his hair.

"Sorry for keeping you so long, Blondie," he said. "I really did drink too much."

He got up and dressed without further comment. Laura slipped back into her dress and escorted him out of the building. The street was relatively quiet, and the air was vibrant against their warm skin. The searchlights were off and the sky glistened with stars. It was a vista rarely witnessed by Londoners. The dark shapes of other people passed them in silence as they walked back toward Piccadilly Circus and the Monico Restaurant. Felix, in all likelihood, was already there. When they got to the Eros News Theatre, Laura asked the airman if he would be all right on his own from this point on.

"Of course," he said, taking her hand in his. "I wish you all the best tonight, Blondie. I hope you make lots of money."

With that, he turned and walked away, just another dark shape disappearing into the night.

Felix Sampson stood outside the Monico Restaurant waiting for Gordon Cummins. It was closing in on 11:30 p.m. His time with Molly had lasted barely fifteen minutes, but he had done what he wanted to do. Next on his agenda was to find a late-night club—maybe even another woman—and see the good times through to the early daylight hours. These days, one had to take advantage of such opportunities when one could. There was no time for frivolity at St. James's Close in Regent's Park, where he and Cummins were stationed with three hundred other men.

Some of the other officer trainees looked upon Cummins with a disdainful eye. His aristocratic demeanor and upper-class way of speaking had earned him the semi-derogatory nickname of "Duke." But Felix liked the bloke. Despite the man's snobbish pretensions, he found Cummins an easygoing sort of person who—despite being married—was not afraid of a good time. He knew little of Cummins's personal life, only that he was married to a woman who was secretary to some theater producer. Felix was married, too, but harbored little guilt over the violation of his vows. When death seems to be one's most likely prospect, moral restraints rather lose their importance. Anyway, it wasn't only men who were cheating. How many of the women working the streets had a man fighting in the scorched deserts of North Africa or venturing over Germany each night in a flying coffin to repay the debt burdening the likes of London and Coventry? For those in need of one, an excuse for just about anything could be found in the popular adage "There's a war on." And so the two men—at Cummins's suggestion—had come to the West End to live it up a little. Felix had originally demurred on the offer because of financial concerns, but was easily swayed that morning when Cummins pulled out a wallet fat with cash.

"Christ, how much is that?" Felix had asked.

"Twenty-one pounds," Cummins replied, flipping through the stash of notes.

"Where did you get it?"

"Repayment on a debt," Cummins said and offered no further explanation.

The two men had been dismissed at 5:15 p.m. They retreated to the showers and washed, shaved, and splashed on cologne. They left their room together and signed their names in the booking-out book in the billet's lounge. The on-duty guard gave both men their leave passes, and off on their adventure they went. But now it seemed Cummins was missing in action. Felix looked at his watch and saw he had been waiting for nearly twenty-five minutes. The time was midnight, a clear violation of their 10:30 p.m. curfew. But when breaking the rules, one might as well go all out. "Sod him," Felix thought. On an evening such as this, time was too precious a commodity to waste just hanging about. Besides, standing in one place for too long could be dangerous: Who knew when a bomb with your name on it was going to fall from the sky? He took one last look up and down the street, squinting into the darkness, and decided to finish the evening without his cohort—wherever the hell he was.

Evelyn Oatley preferred the company of older men. They were less inclined to be overly aggressive in bed. Their sexual curiosities had been satisfied, and they were not prone to making strange requests or bending her body in ways for which it was not designed. On the night of Monday, February 9, the pickings were slim. She was sitting at the bar in the King's Arms pub on Gerrard Street, drinking scotch—her liquor of preference. She drank a lot, though it was not the result of an addiction. She drank to numb the loneliness that constantly consumed her. She longed for meaningful human contact. Beyond the physical sense, she sought to make a true emotional connection with someone, but wondered if she was still capable of having feelings of such depth. Her experiences on the street had left her empty inside and cynical of the intentions of men. At times, she missed her husband. He was a simple man, but a hard worker with a kind heart. On their wedding night, he knew she wasn't a virgin. She had told him shortly after they met that she'd had a child several years before. The child had since been adopted and taken to Canada.

They had married on June 25, 1936, four years after they met in the bleak seaside resort of Blackpool. When they made each other's acquaintance, she was a member of the chorus line at London's notorious Windmill Theatre, where the girls came on stage naked but were not allowed to move, and which after the war was able to boast, "We never closed!" Soon, however, she abandoned the stage to join her husband on his poultry farm up north. For eighteen months she worked alongside him, before tiring of country life. She missed London and the neon dazzle of the West End. They had married on the condition that should she grow bored of rural living, he would let her return to the city. He kept his word and stood in the doorway of their modest cottage and watched her leave. Within weeks of her return to the capital, she sent him a letter saying she had found a place to live. She was still hoping to make it as an actress, but the outbreak of war changed everything. Her husband's poultry farm went under, and opportunities for the stage dried up. She turned to the streets to make money. Even when she admitted to her husband, at the end of 1941, what she was doing, his affection for her remained strong.

There was little affection, however, to be found in the company she now kept. But she tried to make her clients spend the night. She was scared to sleep alone. The barman's shout of "Last call!" derailed her thoughts. She finished her drink and stepped outside in search of business. Wearing a black dress, black coat and black hat, she blended well with the night. She loitered here and there before eventually walking to the Monico Restaurant. Some of the other girls were there, including Marjorie and Big Violet. She joined them for a cigarette.

"Evelyn, how's things?" said a voice behind her. She turned and saw it was another working girl she knew only as Ann.

"Quiet," Evelyn said.

A couple of Canadian soldiers hovered nearby, checking out the selection. One of them—wearing khaki battle dress and a trench coat—gave Evelyn a salacious look of approval. He had on his head one of those funny little caps that all soldiers seemed to wear at a precarious angle. She liked the way they looked—and she liked the look of the airman's cap, too, when he approached her a short time later. He was handsome, with an accent that hinted at weekends in the country and afternoon drives in the Rolls. He had a slim but powerful build and his hair stuck out from underneath his cap in a scruffy manner. His smile dazzled, even in the darkness. Although he was younger than Evelyn preferred, she found him charming.

When she inquired as to his likes, he responded: "I like blondes."

Ivy Poole had spent her evening at the Phoenix Theatre on Shaftsebury Avenue. She returned to her building shortly before 10:30 p.m. and walked up the stairs to her flat. She could tell Evelyn was out, because her neighbor's door was closed and there were no sounds coming from the adjoining apartment. Ivy turned on her wireless, and the sounds of big-band music filled the cramped living space. She stood idly for a moment then decided to wash her hair.

She grabbed an empty pitcher from her cupboard and left

the flat. She went up one flight of stairs to the single bath-room shared by the building's three tenants. She filled the pitcher and returned to her flat, where she poured the water into the kettle and turned on the stovetop. She washed her hair over a large bowl and—in a moment of spontaneity—decided to add a little tint. This she did to the continuing strains of Glenn Miller and Benny Goodman that came and went in waves of static. As she rubbed her hair dry with a towel, the music show ended and the European news came on. At 11 p.m., Ivy took a seat at the table and listened to the broadcast. British forces were slugging it out in a back-and-forth campaign against the Germans and Italians in North Africa. The influx of American troops to Great Britain con-tinued in the wake of Pearl Harbor and the German declara-tion of war upon the United States. The first boatload of Yanks had arrived on January 26. The Japanese were making gains in the Pacific.

The news continued for roughly forty minutes. When it concluded, Ivy turned the wireless off and heard the street-entrance door downstairs open and close. Stepping into the hallway, she flicked on the stairwell light to see who had entered the building. It was Evelyn.

"Thanks," Evelyn said.

A man who appeared to be in his mid-twenties followed Evelyn up the stairs. He had the fresh complexion of youth and, except for his mustache, appeared clean-shaven. His hair, chestnut brown and wavy in the front, was parted on the left, but wild and frizzy on the crown. His hands were thrust deep in the pockets of his overcoat, which was light blue, square at the shoulders and seemed to be tailor-made. A belt around the waist of the coat hung open down at his sides. The coat itself was buttoned up to the collar, which he had up around his neck with the points of the lapels sticking out. Ivy estimated the man stood about five feet, eight inches tall. He said nothing to her as he walked past her into Evelyn's apartment. His face was thin and one of sharp angles. His chin protruded slightly. Evelyn gave Ivy a knowing smile as she disappeared with the man into her apartment and shut the door.

Ivy went back to her place and continued prettying herself up. She could hear Evelyn's voice and that of the man's coming through the wall. The sounds came to Ivy as a semi-intelligible muffle, for, as usual, Evelyn had turned on her wireless. Ivy finished tinting her hair and went to the stove to make a cup of tea. She waited for the water to boil then sat with her cat and sipped the brew. She could still hear the muffled voices and the sounds of Evelyn's wireless beyond the wall. The midnight news was just beginning. She could make out the trim and proper voice of the BBC announcer reading some bulletin from the Pacific theater. The news broadcast ended at quarter past the hour and was followed by a music program. Ivy got up from the table and began getting ready for bed. The time was 12:20 a.m. on Tuesday, February 10.

Ivy climbed into bed and settled her head on the pillow. She was just drifting off when the sound of loud music pulled her with a sudden jerk from the brink of unconsciousness. Next door, someone had turned Evelyn's wireless up as loud as it would go. Although she often listened to music late into the night, never did Evelyn play it at such an inconsiderate volume. Ivy considered knocking on her neighbor's door, but the thought of Evelyn and her male companion in the midst of a naked embrace quickly pushed the idea from her head. She lay back on her pillow and forced her eyes closed. The sound of big-band horns and rollicking piano continued for quite a while before someone—Ivy supposed Evelyn—turned it down. The wireless muted, Ivy closed her eyes and drifted away, not realizing a scene of horror was unfolding a few feet from where she lay.

FEBRUARY 10, 1942

THREE

On Tuesday morning, detectives returned to the bomb shelter with a picture of the strangled woman in hand. They knocked on doors and showed the photograph to people who winced at the brutality of it, but shook their heads when asked if they knew her identity. Time and again they were met with quizzical gazes and shrugged shoulders. The break came when Detective Inspector John Freshney knocked on the front door of a boardinghouse—the Three Arts Club—at 76 Gloucester Place, just a short distance from where the body had been found. Catherine Jones, the manageress, opened the door.

Freshney showed Jones the photograph and asked her if she had seen the woman before. Jones's face registered a look of shocked recognition as she took the photograph from Freshney's hand.

"She came and rented a room the other day," Jones said.

Freshney pulled out a notepad. "What was her name?"

"Evelyn Hamilton."

Jones said the woman checked in at about 10:30 p.m. two days prior, went up to her room, then came down twenty minutes later and asked if there was anywhere to eat dinner at such a late hour. Jones said she told Hamilton that the nearby Lyon's Corner House at Marble Arch, on the west end of Oxford Street, usually served late meals.

"I know she was wearing a light-colored coat," Jones said. "I thought she was wearing a scarf on her head, but it may have been a woolen hat or turban affair. She left and didn't come back."

Freshney nodded and asked Jones if she would come to the mortuary to identify the body. Jones said yes, and at 10:30 a.m. she found herself in the cold surroundings of the morgue. The place reeked of chemicals and antiseptic. As Freshney—accompanied by Clare—looked on, Spilsbury wheeled out the body and pulled back a white sheet, revealing the lifeless features beneath.

Jones nodded.

"That's her," she said. "That's Miss Evelyn Hamilton."

Freshney and Clare drove Jones back to her house and proceeded to Lyon's Corner House at Marble Arch. With four floors and multiple dining rooms—each one with a different theme and live band playing—Lyon's was not your typical dining establishment. Inside, a massive tea bar ran the length of the first floor. Behind the bar, big copper cauldrons stretched from floor to ceiling, with gurgling steam pipes jutting from their sides. It was from these contraptions the tea was served. Ornate stools lined the bar, on which were placed cups and saucers ready for use.

The windows were crossed with tape to prevent them

from exploding into a million pieces of jagged shrapnel should a bomb detonate nearby. On the walls were the typical propaganda posters distributed by the Ministry of Information. "Careless Talk Costs Lives," read one. It showed two businessmen sitting on a train, lost in deep conversation. On the seat behind them sat a sinister little Nazi, scribbling furiously into a notebook. Another poster showed an elegant woman reclining on a sofa. A suave-looking gentleman stood nearby. "Be Like Dad," it read, "Keep Mum." Beneath the posters, booths lined the walls, and tables and chairs crowded the center floor. Waitresses in crisply pressed uniforms ran back and forth with trays in their hands. The girls at Lyon's were known for their incredibly speedy service. The rapidity with which they brought food to the customers had earned them the nickname "Nippies."

The place thrummed with the casual sounds of dining, a far cry from the world outside with its crumbling buildings and bomb-cratered roads. Beyond the walls of the restaurant, the war was everywhere. Unsightly barrage balloons—massive zeppelin-shaped bulks—hovered over the city and obscured the sky near potential enemy targets. Green canvas sandbags were piled up around lampposts and building entrances as a precautionary measure against German incendiaries. Emergency pontoon bridges stretched across the Thames, and brick bomb shelters—like the one Evelyn Hamilton had been found in—cluttered the sidewalks. The Victoria Embankment bristled with pillboxes, ready to be used in the event of a German landing. One such box on New Bridge Street had been built to resemble the entrance to one of London's underground stations, complete with newspaper placards.

Some government buildings and other vital targets were encircled by tangled perimeters of barbed wire. Throughout the city, antiaircraft batteries pointed skyward in anticipation of nightfall and the bombers that might come. Night after night, the people of London were forced to seek cover in the city's subway or retreat to their backyard shelters as the Luftwaffe descended. The raids were a terrifying cacophony of noise, sometimes lasting up to six hours. Air-raid sirens screamed and the city's antiaircraft guns roared as they threw fire into the sky. The cannonade of bombs thundered through the city, as did the sound of its buildings falling, the wail of fire engines and the drone of enemy bombers. In the subway, people crowded on the platforms in their sleeping bags and blankets. They clogged escalators and took up every inch of free space. Some people staked out a place for their family during the day and stood guard over it. Sanitation was poor. People slept crammed up against one another, whether they knew the person or not. Bathing was not possible every day, as bombs often severed gas and water mains. The vast majority of the besieged population endured the assaults in a stoic manner. There were sing-alongs in the shelters, organized games and colorful debate. But for others, the raids were a horror too big to cope with, and they descended into a screaming madness.

In the summer of 1939, as war clouds gathered over Europe, the British government encouraged people to buy bomb shelters for their homes. Some reinforced their garages and cellars with sandbags, or built brick shelters in their gardens. It was not wholly uncommon for a family to be wiped out in its entirety when a homemade shelter took a direct hit. Most Londoners had little faith in open-trench shelters, such as those that now snaked through the grounds of Hyde Park. Some viewed them as ready-made burial ditches. The bombs were indiscriminate in their slaughter. They brought down banks and office buildings, homes and schools. Once the all clear sounded, people emerged to a morbid scene—one of wafting smoke and devastation. Fire hoses lined flooded streets as overworked fire brigades fought the flames, and rescue squads sifted through rubble in search of the dead and wounded. Behind the scenes, undertakers scurried to make sure enough coffins were on hand.

The bustling dining room of Lyon's seemed far removed from the grim world outside. Freshney and Clare maneuvered between the tables, where diners sat with their gas masks—conveniently carried in what appeared to be brown parcels with string handles attached—at their feet. Most people feared a gas attack more than routine bombing. The London County Council distributed a leaflet titled *Anti-Gas Precautions for Civil Defence*, which warned a nervous public that mustard gas smelt somewhat like horseradish. Despite these fears, many people remained lackadaisical when it came to lugging a bulky gas mask around.

But now, they were merely engaged in the civil act of lunch. It seemed to Freshney that people clung to the small things to maintain some sense of normalcy and sanity. But what passed for food these days was hardly normal. Salt cod and soya link sausages were looked upon with much disgust. Meats of questionable origin were sometimes served with few questions as to what was actually in them. Swede and root vegetables seemed to be the main ingredient in every wartime recipe. Rationing had made the acquisition of dairy products, meat and things with sugar difficult. Times were hard for the meat-and-potato man.

The detectives called to a young waitress carrying a loaded tray. Clare introduced himself and Freshney with a flash of his badge. He asked the girl if she was serving tables on the night of February 8, and she said yes. Clare showed the girl a picture of Evelyn Hamilton's clothes, and the picture taken in the morgue. He asked her if she recognized the woman.

"I recognize the woman and the clothes," the waitress said. "She came in here Sunday night. The time was about midnight, and she was alone looking for a seat."

"Did you serve her?" Clare asked.

"No, she didn't sit in my section," the girl said. "I'm not even sure what time she left the restaurant."

"Did she have a meal here?"

"I'm not sure," the girl said.

"What was on your menu Sunday night?" Clare asked.

The girl creased her forehead in concentration and recited Sunday night's culinary choices—including beetroot.

Outside, Clare and Freshney turned up the collars of their coats. The two men were no closer to identifying Evelyn Hamilton's killer, but they now had a reference of time. She was killed while walking back to the boardinghouse from the restaurant. Clare's thoughts turned to the watch on Hamilton's wrist. It had stopped at one o'clock. The time fit with the scenario, which he now played out in his head.

Evelyn Hamilton had arrived at the Three Arts Club on Sunday, February 8, at 10:30 p.m. According to Catherine Jones, the manageress, Hamilton checked into her room and came back downstairs some twenty minutes later in search of a place to eat. She left the house and never returned. Her travel case—which had since been turned over to investigators—contained nothing of any significance beyond clothing. A luggage tag on the bag simply read "E. Hamilton." So, she'd walked from 76 Gloucester Place to Lyon's Corner House at Marble Arch, arriving sometime about midnight. Did she stop along the way? Why did it take her more than an hour to walk a distance of no more than a mile or so? Once at Lyon's, she got a table and ordered a meal, as evidenced by the large amount of beetroot found in her stomach during the postmortem. The waitresses at Lyon's, known for their speed, would have brought the meal quickly, so she was probably in and out within forty minutes. She had been accosted on Montague Place walking back to the boardinghouse, but no one in the area heard any screams that night.

The killer had moved quickly, grabbing her throat and crushing the fragile bones in her neck before she could utter a sound. Had he followed her out of the restaurant, or did he pick up her trail as she walked alone in the dark? There had been a slight scuffle as evidenced by the scratches on her shoes, but her self-defense had been far from vigorous. As Hamilton's body went limp, her assailant bundled her sagging mass into the shelter. Spilsbury had found no evidence of rape, but her clothing had been disarranged and a breast exposed. Had something or someone scared the killer away? Although Clare now knew the victim's movements on that fateful night, he still lacked insight into Evelyn Hamilton herself. Who was she, and what had brought her to London? They were questions being tackled that very moment by detectives at the Marylebone Police Station. Phone calls were being made and family members tracked down, as investigators sought to construct a more precise picture of the victim.

Meanwhile, in another part of town, a second gruesome discovery was about to be made.

Charles Fuelling and George Carter, meter readers with the Central London Electric Company, arrived at 153 Wardour Street at 8 a.m. to collect money from the meters. They knocked on the building's door and waited for an answer. Upstairs, Ivy Poole had just commenced her morning ritual of brewing a cup of tea and flipping through the paper. She hadn't been up long. Judging from the silence next door, Evelyn wasn't up at all. The knock on the door downstairs came just as Ivy placed a bowl of food down for her cat. Still clad in her nightgown, she was loath to answer it, but not wanting Evelyn disturbed, she braved facing the visitor without proper preparation. She went downstairs and opened the door to two workmen clad in overalls.

"Morning, luv," said one. "Here to collect on the meters."

"Oh, certainly," Ivy said. "Do come in."

Coin-operated meters supplied electricity in each apartment. Tenants dropped coins in the meter's slot, turned a dial and—depending on how much they deposited—received a certain amount of time to run the lights and heat. Ivy led the men up the stairs to her flat and let them in. They emptied her meter and asked if anyone else lived in the building.

"There's a gentleman who lives upstairs and a girl who lives next door," Ivy said. "I'll check—she might be asleep."

The three of them went to Evelyn's front door, which faced out above the stairs. Ivy knocked lightly and was surprised when the door swung slowly in on its hinges.

"Are you there, dear?" she asked, knocking again. "Dear, are you home?"

Evelyn's flat was dark, and the silence therein seemed oppressive. Ivy hesitated at the door. Carter placed a reassuring hand on her shoulder and stepped past her into the small room. It was hard to make anything out. The black-out curtains were still draped across the window. In that darkness, a sudden—and rather discomforting—certainty overcame the utility man. He pulled his electric torch from his tool belt and illuminated the room with a pallid beam of light. Ivy and Fuelling huddled close behind him. Carter shone his torch on the dark shape of the bed against the wall. What they saw sent them running from the apartment, down the stairs and into the street.

Their timing coincided with the patrol of Police Inspector John Hennessy, who had been making his morning rounds on Wardour Street. His initial satisfaction that all was quiet deteriorated with the screaming pleas of the two men and a woman running toward him. George Carter reached him first. Out of breath and trying to find the words to explain the panic, Carter blurted: "We just found a dead woman at 153 Wardour." Now, with Hennessy following closely behind, the meter men and Ivy Poole ran back to the building. Just shy of 8:40 a.m., the four of them climbed the stairs to the landing outside Evelyn Oatley's flat. Hennessy told the other three to stay put. With electric torch in hand he entered the flat, mindful not to disturb anything. Heavy shadow cloaked the room, and in the morbid glow of his torch, Hennessy saw a young woman—her throat slashed—draped across the bed. Rammed up inside of her, the handle of her own flashlight protruded from between her thighs.

Hennessy came out of the bedroom and spoke to Fuelling.

"You're going to have to help on this," he said. "Go to Trenchard House and have a message sent to West End Central Station. Tell them a divisional surgeon and a divisional detective inspector are needed at these premises immediately."

Hennessy would normally have carried out this mission himself, but as no other police officers were present, it was imperative he guard the crime scene against any further intrusion. After watching Fuelling run down the stairs and

out into the street, he turned to George Carter and Ivy
Poole and took their statements. Before he had finished,
Alexander Baldie, the divisional surgeon, arrived on scene.
At 8:50 a.m., Baldie walked to the bed and gave the body a
cursory glance. To enable him to see, he opened the blackout curtains. A dismal gray light flooded the room and fell
across the body. The pale white skin of the woman's neck
lay open in a wide, red gash. Being careful not to disturb
the body more than need be, he gently raised the woman's
right arm. Rigor mortis extended down to the elbow. The
woman's torso was nearly cold, hardly surprising since the
room's temperature was almost the same as that outside.
An accurate time of death was hard to come by based on
such a limited examination. But running through his mind
the formulas and calculations of his trade, Baldie concluded that the woman had been dead for no more than
three or four hours.

Less than ten minutes after Baldie's arrival, Detective
Inspector Clarence Jeffery of the West End Central Station, "C" Division, entered the apartment. Baldie shared
with Jeffery his theory surrounding the time of death. The
inspector made note of it and began recording the details
of the crime scene. The woman lay diagonally across the
bed. A pillow was on the floor beneath her head, which
hung over the edge of the bed. A bloodstained Ever Ready
safety razor blade lay on the blankets to the left of her
head. Next to it there lay a blood-smeared pair of curling
tongs, while a bloody tin opener rested between her legs.
Blood covered the white metal handle of the flashlight
protruding from her vagina. The woman's eyes stared
blankly off into eternity. A considerable amount of blood
had flowed from her neck and onto the floor, where it ran
in a thickening stream about five feet in length across the

room. There were a number of superficial cuts near the woman's pubic region. The bed, which was really no more than a divan, was fully made and showed no signs of being slept in.

Jeffery called for Hennessy and asked him to put through an urgent call to Superintendent Cherrill of the Fingerprint Department and Detective Inspector Law of the Photograph Section. As Hennessy walked out, Divisional Detective Inspector Charles Gray walked in and assumed control of the scene. Looking around the room, Gray noticed the door on the wardrobe—situated between the divan and the electric fireplace—had been forced open. The lock lay on the bed and floor in two broken pieces. Inside the wardrobe, Gray found two knives, two forks and two spoons. A black leather handbag rested on a sofa, which faced the fireplace. The bag's contents—a leather wallet, two Post Office Savings Bank Books in the name of Evelyn Oatley and several letters—were strewn messily about. The wallet, like the bag, was open, and Gray could see there was no money in either. On the small nightstand beside the bed were the wireless set and seven Gillette safety razor blades.

A washbasin stood against the wall near the wardrobe. On it, Gray saw a box containing an Ever Ready safety razor and a safety razor blade of the same brand. He ordered that they be bagged as evidence once the crime scene had been photographed. The victim's black coat, which hung from the wardrobe, would also be collected. Draped across the back of an easy chair were a black dress, a slip, a brassiere, a pair of stockings and a skirt. These would be analyzed at the lab, along with the woman's tweed jacket, which hung from the back of a chair near the fireplace. There were two keys on the mantelpiece. A quick experiment by Gray showed they fit the Yale-brand locks that secured the door to Evelyn's room and the street-level door to the building.

Gray took another look at the body. In life, he thought, she must have been quite pretty.

Following a debauched evening of whoring and drinking it up, Air Cadet Felix Sampson returned to his billet at St. James's Close at 6 a.m. When Gordon Cummins failed to meet up with him again the previous night, Sampson had continued the party on his own. At the street entrance to an underground station in Piccadilly Circus, he had met another woman who made it be known that her services were available for a fair price. She was a good-looking sort, and far from being tired, Sampson had taken her up on the offer. The time had been midnight. He followed her down the stairs into the underground, where she bought tickets for them both. They boarded a train and got off at a station, the name of which Sampson would eventually forget. They had gone to the woman's flat and worked her bedsprings in spectacular fashion. It was not until 5:30 a.m.—some three hours before the chilling discovery at Wardour Street—that he crawled out of the woman's flat and staggered back to the billet in the unkind light of day.

His bunk was in Flat 27, which he shared with six other men going through the RAF's officer-training program. Not wanting to draw the ire of the guard in the lobby—who would undoubtedly be fuming over a certain missing signature in the sign-in book for the previous evening—Sampson opted to enter the billet via the fire escape. He walked around to the side of the building and ascended the metal stairs to the second floor, where he climbed through an open window into the bunk quarters. His six other bunkmates were in bed, including Cummins. He sneaked up to Cummins's bunk and knelt down beside it, shaking Cummins on the shoulder. Cummins groaned lightly and opened a bloodshot eye.

"When did you get in?" Sampson asked.

"Three-thirty."

"Have you booked in?"

"No. Have you?"

"No," Sampson whispered. "What are we going to do?"

Cummins didn't answer—he had drifted back to sleep. Sampson shook his friend's shoulder again.

"What?"

"What happened to you last night? Why didn't you come back to meet me?"

"The woman I went with didn't satisfy me," Cummins said, "so I went and found someone else."

And with that, he rolled onto his other side and presented Sampson with his back. Sampson got up and lurched toward his own bunk, overcome by the previous night's cheap booze and easy sex. He undressed—not bothering to fold his clothes or place them in his footlocker at the end of the bunk—and climbed into bed. Reveille sounded less than an hour later. By the time Sampson, Cummins and the other cadets in Flat 27 ate breakfast, showered and completed morning drills, Chief Superintendent Frederick Cherrill of Scotland Yard was on the way to his second murder scene in as many days.

When Frederick Cherrill joined the Fingerprint Department in 1920, it was situated on the top floor of the red-and-white gothic-style headquarters of the Metropolitan Police Department on Victoria Embankment. The entire bureau was housed in a single room that overlooked the

Thames. The view of the city and its ancient river could be seen through a circular window dubbed the "Bull's Eye," because of its resemblance to the crosshairs of a riflescope. Cherrill still had the odd occasion to walk past the "Bull's Eye" and, when he did, his mind wandered back to those early days. War had changed the view of the city dramatically. The once majestic panorama of the metropolis now looked like a mouth of shattered teeth, and the sky was often red with fire or black with smoke. The work had changed, too, growing in scope and becoming ever more complex. By the time Cherrill assumed the position of the Fingerprint Department's chief superintendent in 1938, the bureau had moved to a newly built annex next door to the main building. Now it occupied multiple rooms lined with filing cabinets and bookshelves, housing a catalog of hundreds of thousands of prints.

Cherrill had just reached his office at Scotland Yard that morning when he received Hennessy's message. He immediately donned his bowler and departed for the Wardour Street address. The brutality of the crime shocked him when he arrived at the scene. He made a minute examination of the room and its contents. In the open handbag that was lying on the sofa, Cherrill saw a piece of mirror. He ordered it bagged as evidence, along with the bloodied tin opener and the curling tongs. A close inspection of the room's furniture revealed no bloody markings, and there was nothing discernible in the blood that flowed across the floor from the bed to the wall. At 12:30 p.m., as Cherrill roamed the apartment, examining everything through his magnifying glass, Sir Bernard Spilsbury arrived. The body, thus far, had been touched by no one but Baldie.

Spilsbury knelt at the side of the bed as he pulled on a pair of surgical gloves. His face expressionless, he made note of the evident cuts and slashes to the body. The flash-light protruding from the woman's vagina had been pushed about four inches up inside her. Gently, he slipped a gloved hand under her back. The skin there was warm, but the rest of her body was cold. There was heavy bruising around her neck. Kneeling by the woman's head, Spilsbury shone a light into her eyes. There was hemorrhaging on the whites of her eyes and in her eyelids. He pulled back her gums with a delicate finger and saw that the tissue of her mouth was flushed with blood.

"There was an attempt at manual strangulation before the throat was cut," Spilsbury said to Gray. "Look at the abrasions on the front of the neck and the signs of hemor-rhaging in the eyes and mouth."

Spilsbury pointed to the puncture wounds near the woman's pubic hair. "These bled little," he said. "They were probably inflicted when she was on the verge of death after the cut to the neck. I'll know more after a full postmortem."

Gray nodded and ordered that the body be taken to the Westminster Mortuary.

As Inspector Gray looked on, Spilsbury donned his leather apron and assembled an array of tools for cutting and probing. Evelyn Oatley lay stretched out before him, her positioning now more natural than the one in which she was found on the bed. The pathologist said nothing as he pulled on a pair of gloves and slid a hand between her thighs. Slowly, he removed the flashlight—approximately six inches in length—and secured it in an evidence bag. It would have to be checked for fingerprints. Spilsbury then measured the body, which he noted was well nourished and well developed, for height. She was five feet, two inches tall. He made a note of the measurement before inspecting her neck. Against Evelyn's pale white skin, the trauma inflicted by the killer stood out in startling red contrast. Across the front of her throat—chiefly on the right side—was a jagged gash nearly six inches long. Spilsbury carefully probed the wound, pulling back the skin to get a clearer view of the damage done. The large vein of the neck had been severed. From this external observation, it seemed the cut had penetrated all the way to the back of the throat. Four superficial wounds surrounded the slash, and about two inches below these were a number of superficial abrasions. A large bruise discolored the inner right side of the woman's lower lip. Moving down the body, there were twelve cuts in the external genital area. Half of these were made in the region of her pubic hair. The six remaining wounds were around the orifice of the vagina. The injuries were ragged and appeared to have been inflicted with the tip of the tin opener found at the scene.

Internally, there was hemorrhaging in the scalp and at the top of the head. With his scalpel, Spilsbury cut a large "Y" into the dead woman's flesh. Two separate incisions started at the tip of each shoulder and converged just above the midpoint of the chest, between her breasts. From there, he made a long incision down to the navel. He peeled back the skin and sawed through the bone. The internal organs appeared healthy but congested. There was a minute amount of blood in the passages of both ears, and hemorrhaging in the lining of the larynx. Bruising was evident on both sides of the tongue. The tonsils and the glands in the upper portion of the neck were engorged with blood. In the stomach, there remained a small amount of food that had been partially digested. Some blood was present in the vagina, but there was no trace of semen. Because the bleeding in the vagina had been minimal, Spilsbury opined that the flashlight had been inserted into the victim after death. The blood that was present was in all likelihood carried in by the flashlight. There were no defensive wounds on the hands, or skin under the nails, and Spilsbury deduced that the woman was unconscious from the attempted strangulation when her attacker slit her throat.

"The cause of death was major hemorrhaging from the neck," Spilsbury said to Gray. "Judging from the appearance of the wound, I would guess the razor blade you found was used in cutting the throat. The first act was that of strangulation, which was continued until she was unconscious. Her throat was then cut in the position in which she was found with her head hanging over the side of the bed."

Spilsbury pointed between the woman's thighs.

"The wounds about the external genital area were inflicted whilst she was alive but at the point of death," he said. "The electric torch was then pushed up the vagina, carrying blood from these wounds. Although the razor was probably used to cut the neck, the wounds to the genital area were inflicted by a blunt cutting edge. I think, perhaps, the tin opener was used in this area."

Cherrill sat in his office with the bloody accoutrements taken from Evelyn Oatley's apartment spread out before him. Ready to be examined were the tin opener, the razor blade and the curling tongs. The piece of mirror found lying in the poor woman's handbag also lay on his worktable. Cherrill wondered how many times the young lady had stared into her looking glass to fix her eyeliner or lipstick. He placed the piece of mirror in front of him and studied it through his magnifying glass. Almost immediately he saw against the glass in one corner the faint swirls of what he knew to be a thumbprint. With a feather brush, he applied a thin application of black powder to increase the print's contrast against the mirror. He used a small piece of lifting tape to capture the print and stuck it on an index card. A comparison with the dead woman's prints taken in the morgue ruled out a match. The killer himself must have left the print on the glass when he rummaged through the handbag. Cherrill's pulse quickened at the prospect of a lead as he reached for the tin opener. He passed his feather brush over the opener's handle and frosted the tarnished metal with powder. A series of prints quickly became evident. Cherrill put the brush down and passed his magnifying glass over his handiwork. He swallowed hard at what he saw.

The prints had been made by a left-handed individual.

The idea that one and the same person might be responsible for the murder of Evelyn Oatley and Evelyn Hamilton had not yet been considered. The crime scenes had offered little in way of similarities. Evelyn Hamilton had been strangled. Evelyn Oatley had suffered a violent stab wound to her neck and had been sexually violated with an inanimate object. Cherrill looked again at the prints on the handle. They had definitely been made by a left hand and were not in a position that would have resulted from using the opener for its intended purpose. Cherrill reexamined the impression on the piece of mirror. Its diagonal placement on the glass suggested that it, too, had been made by a left-handed person. He licked his lips as he excitedly pondered the possibility of finding a match in the Yard's print index. Since 1930, the Metropolitan Police Department had employed a recording system of single fingerprints. This eased the burden placed on an investigator trying to find a match. As opposed to all ten fingerprints being filed together, prints were now cataloged individually in ten separate collections. Prints of the right thumb were stored in No. 1 collection, followed by prints of the right forefinger in No. 2 collection. The numbered collections progressed to their obvious conclusion: No. 10 collection, in which were cataloged prints of the little finger of the left hand.

Finding a match still posed a great challenge. After lifting prints from a crime scene or piece of evidence, an investigator had to determine which finger had left which specific prints. This was generally done through an examination of finger positioning and deducing how fingers fell across a certain object when grasped. It was the same approach used by Cherrill in determining the left-handed nature of the man whose prints were on the tin opener and piece of mirror. Once an investigator knew which finger had left a print, he could begin his search through the Yard's print index. If it was determined that a print had been made by the third finger of someone's right hand, a search of No. 3 collection would begin. The collections, in turn, were categorized according to what sort of crimes the prints were associated with. Of course, finding a match depended on the quality of the print. Perfect impressions were a rarity. Prints left in the midst of some violent act often were smeared or incomplete, requiring great skill on the part of the investigator to ascertain their characteristics.

The depiction of fingerprint detection in novels of mystery and suspense was a constant source of amusement for Cherrill. In a gothic English manor far removed from civilization on the desolate moors, at a party attended by distinguished guests, someone plunges a knife into the colonel's back. The murder arouses much fear among those gathered, who focus their suspicions on the butler. Eventually, out from the city, comes the detective from Scotland Yard. He scours the scene of the crime and finds a set of unblemished prints on the handle of the knife protruding from the colonel's back. Another perfect set is lifted from a tumbler on the nearby wet bar. Questions are asked, alibis are checked and motives explored. But it's the fingerprints that eventually point to the guilty party—and, just as everyone suspected, it's the butler. Such naive oversimplification made Cherrill laugh. While a matched fingerprint could undisputedly prove a person was at a certain location, it offered no indication as to when that individual was there. Certainly, the butler's fingerprints would be on the knife handle and the glass. If he lived or worked on the premises, one would expect to find his prints on such things. In short, fingerprints were just one small piece of a larger puzzle that had to be completed to attain the full picture.

If there was indeed a match in the Yard's index to the prints on the broken piece of mirror and the tin opener, it would certainly point investigators in the right direction—but it wouldn't offer a concrete solution to the crime. Cherrill again examined the items in front of him. The print on the mirror did not match any on the tin opener. In the old days—when the bureau was housed on the top floor of the gothic building next door with its bull's-eye window—prints were stored in a long chest of drawers. By the time the bureau made the move to its current location in the newly built annex, the chest was falling apart. Once the bureau had settled into its new location, Cherrill learned that the old piece of furniture had subsequently been thrown out for firewood. Being one of sentimental disposition, he dreaded the thought of that chest, which he had spent so many years staring at, going up in smoke. He retrieved it and took it to his house in Mitcham. It now stood in his living room and served its purpose as a finely restored bookcase. On its shelves, however, were not books of murder and detection, but volumes on fishing—one of Cherrill's great passions. He supposed that was one of the reasons he enjoyed working with fingerprints. Searching the Yard's index for a match was a fishing expedition of sorts.

The fact that no two people shared the same fingerprint was an unarguable fact. The chance of one person having two fingers sharing the exact same print was, for the purpose of practical thinking, beyond the realm of possibility. Cherrill had read somewhere that American scientists had relegated the chance of such a thing happening to a septillion to one—septillion being a number followed by twenty-four zeros. The outrageousness of the figure never failed to intrigue Cherrill. At one point, he had sat down at his desk in an attempt to get a better grasp on the number's astronomical nature. He eventually determined—after spending some time on his mathematical equations—that if a man picked up a pencil and made three marks with it every second of his life, by the time he had a septillion marks he would—assuming he was blessed with immortality—find himself living in a year far beyond 8,001,900.

Cherrill smirked at the outrageousness of it and turned his attention to the rows of filing cabinets housing the Yard's fingerprint catalog. Police departments all over the country forwarded fingerprints to the Yard following the apprehension of a suspect. The prints were categorized on a special form, which also included the suspect's name, the offense for which he or she had been arrested and the name of the court where the suspect was scheduled to appear. Investigators at the Yard then cross-referenced the newly received prints with those already on file. If a match was found, then details of the previous criminal history were forwarded to the arresting police department. If no previous criminal history existed, the prints were classified and filed in the index. Should the suspect be found not guilty, all information on file relating to that person was destroyed.

Now, as Cherrill began searching the files, he hoped fate would side with him.

FOUR

Inspector Leonard Clare sat in his office at the Marylebone Police Station and stared at the photographs on his desk. The body of Evelyn Hamilton—captured in black-and-white—lay spread out before him. Her exposed right breast and the disarranged nature of her clothing told Clare he was hunting a sexual sadist. He felt a lingering pity for this woman with whom his acquaintance was limited to the recollections of others and these crime-scene photographs. In the twenty-four hours since Hamilton's body had been found, much work had been done in putting together a composite of her life—a life limited in longevity and social interaction. Detectives had tracked down her younger sister, Kathleen, a thirty-one-year-old nurse in Newcastle who was due in London the following day to identify the body. From Kathleen, police branched out within the cramped confines of Evelyn's existence and pieced together her sad story and the loneliness of her final days.

Evelyn Hamilton—National Registration Identity No. FFXE/226/1—was born on February 8, 1901, and died a single woman without children. She was a qualified pharmacist. She began studying chemistry at Skerry's College, a technical school in Newcastle, at sixteen. At nineteen, she completed her studies and went to work at a local pharmacy as a shop assistant. She worked for two pharmacists over the next four years before obtaining her chemist and druggist diploma from Edinburgh University in October 1938. Her school years were uneventful, and there was no fraternization with boys or close friendships with other girls. About a month after graduation, she obtained a job as a shop manageress at another local pharmacy. She held the job until late 1940 then abruptly left it.

"The only reason I can advance for her leaving this position was that she desired a change," Kathleen Hamilton had told Clare. "As a matter of fact, she had mentioned for a considerable time previously that she would like a change and was in fact seeking one."

In mid-1941, she obtained work with a pharmaceutical company in Leicestershire and traveled the North Country pitching its products to retailers. Despite the time she spent on the road, the job did nothing to satisfy the stimulation she so desperately craved. She stuck with the job for seven months before depression and insomnia wore her down. She resigned her post, returned home to Newcastle and moved back in with her mother. At her sister's advice, Evelyn sought counseling from a doctor at the Newcastle Infirmary. The doctor told her she was overworked and needed to take a tonic. She remained at her mother's place for two months, during which time her mood and health improved greatly. In November 1941, she moved to Surrey to take a job with a hospital. Upon her arrival, she learned that the hospital served the mentally ill, and she resigned within a few days when it became obvious there wasn't much for her to do there.

Throughout all this, Evelyn Hamilton remained unattached.

"I have never known her to court anyone and I do not know any of her friends," Kathleen told Clare. "As far as I know, she has never had a man friend. All her holidays were spent with various fellowships and worker educational societies. All her friends were what I describe as intellectuals, and her one hobby in life was to improve her knowledge and mind on all subjects. She was a keen socialist and studied very deeply the problems connected with this subject."

The last job she held was in a pharmacy on the high street in Hornchurch, Essex. She worked as the store manageress for a weekly wage of five pounds, which she took from the till at the end of each week. Not completely trusting of banks, she carried large sums of money with her. Financial troubles resulting from the war forced the shop to close just weeks before her murder. On the morning of Sunday, February 8, Evelyn Hamilton—who lived in a boardinghouse not far from the shop—settled her lodgings account with her landlady. At 6 p.m. that same day, she left her boarding room. With her, she carried her ration books and identity card. According to the landlady, Mrs. Eva Lever, Evelyn also wore a gold wristwatch when she left. She was next seen about forty minutes later on the high street by a casual acquaintance who knew her as the manageress at the drugstore. Mrs. Maud Yoxall told detectives that Evelyn had with her a small travel case and handbag. Evelyn told Mrs. Yoxall she was leaving for Grimsby—where she had been offered a job at yet another pharmacy—but was planning on spending the night in London.

The deceased's movements remained unaccounted for over the next forty minutes, but Mr. William Whatford—the booking agent at Hornchurch Railway Station—saw her at about 7:20 p.m. She purchased a ticket for London and made arrangements to have luggage picked up from Mrs. Lever's boardinghouse and forwarded to the station in Grimsby, her ultimate destination. The booking agent had her fill out a passenger's luggage-in-advance form and told her the baggage would be collected the following day and dispatched to the luggage office at Grimsby Station.

"I noticed the woman had a peculiar way of speaking, as if there was something wrong with her vocal chords," Whatford told police. "When she filled in the form, I asked her if it was Miss or Mrs. She told me Miss, and this is what I put on the form. The woman also told me she was fed up with this moving about, and she wanted to spend the rest of her days in peace."

Evelyn signed the form and paid for her ticket. She left the booking hall and walked down the stairs to the platform, after which she was next seen at 10 p.m., on Platform 2 at Baker Street Station in London by porter William Parker. He spotted her near the stairs leading up to the street.

"I was approached by a lady passenger who, as far as I can remember, was fifty years of age, of medium height, medium build, and dressed in a small round hat and biscuit-colored coat," Parker told Clare. "She asked me if I could get her a taxi. I told her I wouldn't be sure at that time of night, as it was a Sunday."

Parker—dressed in his dark blue uniform and wearing a peak cap—walked the woman up the stairs, emerging from the lighted underground into the blacked-out world of a city under siege. By sheer luck, a taxi had parked in front of the station. Parker asked the driver if he would take another passenger, and the driver—a Cockney with accent to match—said he would. The porter loaded Evelyn's small travel case into the back of the car and helped her in. She thanked him and slipped some silver into his palm. Parker stood on the pavement momentarily to make sure they got off all right. He could see her silhouette through the taxi's back window and watched as she leaned forward and spoke to the driver. Seconds later, the taxi's engine came to life, and the big black shape of the car vanished into the night.

Parker glanced up at the sky and, out of habit, strained his ears for the drone of approaching bombers. Married, he had a son and a daughter. He and his wife had evacuated the children to Cornwall at the start of the war. It was a torment for parent and child—and one suffered by thousands of families as they packed their children off to the homes of strangers, away from the nightmare of screaming sirens and a burning city. In some strange way, Parker considered him and his wife to be lucky. Some children had been whisked across the oceans to America, Canada, Australia and South Africa. The voyage to distant shores was a hazardous endeavor, and some ships fell prey to roaming packs of U-boats. The Parkers had not been burdened by such a worry. They had put their children on a train bound for the English countryside. Now they were waiting for the bombs to stop falling and for their children to return home. With these thoughts weighing on his mind, Parker walked back down the stairs and took up his position on the platform. He remained on duty until 12:30 a.m. Ten minutes after clocking out, he boarded the staff train leaving Baker Street and took it to Talbot Grove, arriving there at 12:50 a.m. He was in his house on Ladbroke Grove five minutes later.

"I did not make an appointment to meet the woman again," Parker told Clare. "She was a total stranger to me."

His wife confirmed the time of her husband's return home. Parker was obviously not a suspect, but a valuable witness.

Abraham Ash, badge no. 11873, drove the taxi that night. He maneuvered the car carefully through the dark as Evelyn Hamilton sat silently in the backseat. The address she had given him was for a boardinghouse at 28 Gloucester Place, and now she stared passively out the window.

The streets were empty, and the buildings they drove past were black, featureless blocks. The bombings had emblazoned a library of painful images on the national conscience: Broken bodies being pulled from rubble, mothers screaming for their lost children and children screaming for their lost mothers, cars and buses tossed aside like toys, severed limbs being swept up from the gutter. This was not Evelyn's first wartime excursion to London. She thought back to her previous trip the year before and remembered the city's hard mornings. Fires burned and great clouds of black smoke filtered the light of the sun, bathing the city in a depressing gunmetal tint.

The taxi turned onto Gloucester Place and drove slowly past the houses. Evelyn had to use her flashlight to illuminate the numbers on the doors, but the light was weak and flickered on and off. They eventually reached No. 28. Evelyn told Ash to wait a moment. He watched her walk up the stairs and knock on the door. A maid answered, and Ash watched as his passenger and the maid engaged in what seemed to be a heated conversation.

In his statement to Clare, Ash told the inspector: "The woman, who was well spoken, although she spoke slowly, then returned to the cab, slightly perturbed, and said, 'They must put me up somewhere. I have got money to pay for the room.'"

"Where do you want to go in the morning?" Ash asked. "Perhaps we can find a room near where you want to get to."

"I'm going to King's Cross in the morning," the woman told Ash. "From there, I'm going to Grimsby—but I don't want a room in the King's Cross district."

Ash told Clare the woman then asked him to drive her to the Three Arts Club at 76 Gloucester Place. She told the cabbie she had stayed there before. Ash did as the woman asked.

"I turned my cab and drove her there," Ash said in his statement. "She got out and made an enquiry, then went in. She came out after a couple of minutes and said she had got a room. I carried the bag to her and she paid me. She held the handbag to her sides and opened the top outwards. The fare was 1/9d—she paid me 2/6d. I then drove away."

From that point on, Clare knew the story. When questioned about Evelyn Hamilton's previous stay at the Three Arts Club, Catherine Jones—the manageress who first identified the body the previous day—said she had no recollection of Miss Hamilton ever visiting before the night in question. The only thing Mrs. Jones could add was that her guest seemed agitated but didn't say why. After receiving her key, Miss Hamilton put her traveling case in her room and then went out for a late dinner. She never returned. Clare grunted and put Jones's statement aside. He sorted through those of the other witnesses, looking for anything that might have been overlooked. He had performed this exercise countless times over the past twenty-four hours.

He reviewed statements taken from the waitress at Lyon's Corner House and Arthur Cyril Williams, the War Reserve constable who checked the bomb shelters on Montague Place that night as part of his regular beat. There was the

statement of another War Reserve constable, too—Kenneth
Victor Begley, who worked out of the Marylebone Lane Police Station on the night of the murder. Had the killer's identity been even suspected, perhaps Begley's statement would
have attracted more attention than it did.

On the night in question, War Reserve Constable Kenneth Begley patrolled the No. 13 and No. 14 beats, which en-
compassed the north side of Montague Place and areas
north of the Marylebone Road. He commenced duty at midnight on the No. 14 beat. All seemed quiet. The sirens remained blessedly silent and the searchlights were dimmed.
There were some nights when the actual sky seemed to be
on fire; when the East End docks burned and the sky blazed
a vibrant shade of crimson, as if some great artery had been
sliced open and bled through the very fabric of space. But
that was not the case this night. Begley walked at a casual
pace, comfortable with the geography of the blacked-out
streets and mindful of lampposts and sandbags. He took a
one-hour refreshment at Aybrook Street Section House from
2:50 a.m. to 3:50 a.m. and returned to his duties.

Shortly before 5 a.m., two soldiers looking for the
Great Central Hotel approached him in the Marylebone
Road. Begley told them they were only a block away and
pointed them in the right direction. He began patrolling
Montague Place ten minutes later, passing the dark shapes
of the surface shelters on the south side of the street. He
paused on the opposite side of the road and listened for
any noise coming from the squat, brick structures. He heard
nothing and, satisfied, continued on his way. It was not until 5:20 a.m. that he saw the man hurrying toward Baker
Street.

Begley was standing outside the National Registration Offices between Baker and Glentworth streets. He stood with his hands clasped behind his back—ready to render his assistance should it be needed—when he saw the man walking at a rapid pace from the direction of Edgware Road. The western sky surrendered the first faint glimmer of daybreak, and in the burgeoning light Begley could just make out the man's appearance. He stood about five feet, eight inches tall. He boasted a strong but slender build, and it seemed to Begley—who himself measured five feet, eight inches—that the gentleman would prove agile in a fight. The ruffled hair was either blond or light brown. He carried his gas-mask case in one hand and stopped about two yards short of Begley when he caught a glimpse of him.

Begley nodded a silent greeting, and the man did likewise. He approached Begley in a casual manner, his movements having lost the urgency so evident only seconds ago.

"Excuse me," the man said. "But do you know the way to King's Cross?"

The voice was educated, but the refined tone seemed tinged just slightly by a hint of agitation. In his statement to Clare—taken several hours after Evelyn Hamilton's body was discovered—Begley would explain: "When I say agitation, I mean the sort of conversation one would make if one came across anybody unexpectedly after having done something one ought not to have done." This was hardly a circumstance to get overly excited about. London's new dark age was a breeding ground of mischief and crooked activity. Besides, the gentleman had probably done nothing more than frolic with some tart in a side alley and was now feeling guilty for such a sordid misdemeanor. Begley pointed the man in the direction he wanted to go and watched him walk away with an ostentatiously confident swagger, wondering whether the man's privileged upbringing or the dress blues of his RAF uniform accounted for such a strut.

Sitting at his desk, Clare filed Begley's statement with the others. It was time to go home. In the morning, he would have to take Kathleen Hamilton to the morgue to identify her sister.

FIVE

Cherrill's fascination with fingerprints dated back to his early childhood. His family's lineage stretched back generations to the quaint village of Dorchester, on the Thames, near Oxford. It was in Dorchester the young Cherrill grew up, attending classes at the village school and spending his free time hanging about the village workshops, from which artisans had produced goods of iron and wood for centuries. From a young age, Cherrill had a true appreciation for craftsmanship and the art of creating. He would sit for hours and watch the ironworkers bang their hammers on anvils, shaping metal. Down the cobbled street was the woodshop with its sweet fragrance of sawdust and tarnish. He would watch in awe as the men worked in the sawpit amid billows of dust. In later years, Cherrill himself would prove to be adept at woodcarving, the result, he said, of watching the workmen in his village.

When not appreciating the artistry of the village's laborers, Cherrill partook in more boyish pursuits. There were rowdy games with the other boys, pranks played upon girls and occasional mischief in the classroom. The evening hours were spent getting lost in the literary adventures of Detective Sexton Blake. With his curly brimmed bowler and heavy walking stick, Blake was the anti–Sherlock Holmes. Whereas Holmes pontificated and theorized, Blake was a man of action and not deduction. His adversaries were of a more super-villainous caliber, and his escapades took him to far-flung corners of the globe. There were occasions when Cherrill would go to his room to read Blake's latest adventure, only to find the comic missing. His own brief investigation would generally lead him to his father's high-back chair. There, beneath the seat cushion, the young Cherrill would invariably find his missing magazine. His father, when questioned, would simply assure his son he was reading the issue to make sure it was suitable for a young audience. The older Cherrill would relinquish the comic to his son, who would immediately run back upstairs to partake in Blake's latest thrilling endeavor. Cherrill, later in life, would credit Sexton Blake with fueling his own passion for police work.

Cherrill and his father enjoyed a close relationship, and it was from his dad that Cherrill learned the subtleties of angling. On weekends, the two of them—armed with rod and line—wandered down to the Thames to try their luck. They pursued their tranquil hobby in the heart of the English country, where the river cut a torrent of gray through the rolling greenery of Oxfordshire. Not far from where Cherrill and his father fished, the ancient tower of Little Wittenham Church rose above the trees. Sometimes they would forgo the Thames in favor of the gentle stream that passed the old abbey mill nearby. Monks had built the mill in ancient times to grind corn for the neighboring monastery. At the abbey mill one savage December evening, a prophetic event pointed Cherrill in a direction that would eventually lead him to Scotland Yard.

The wind roared down the chimney of the Cherrill family home and fluttered the flames burning in the stone hearth. Cherrill's father sat relaxing in his high-back chair, while young Frederick was lost—yet again—in another Sexton Blake adventure. Occasionally, when a violent gust of wind rattled the windowpanes and made the oak beams creak, he would shift his gaze from the pages of his comic and stare out the window. The world outside was lost in the pitch black and the hard rain that streaked the glass and battered the roof and walls. Cherrill's attention never strayed for long, as Sexton Blake currently found himself in a particularly nasty situation—thanks in no part to an exceptionally deviant fiend. A knock on the door eventually drew the boy away from his story. Wondering who would be out on such a ghastly night, Cherrill's mother opened the door to find the village miller's wife standing on the stoop.

The poor woman was soaked through and out of breath from battling the storm. She came inside and explained that her husband had been bedridden with illness for nearly two weeks. As a result, there was a large surplus of corn that needed grinding. Angry farmers were demanding that someone do it. Cherrill's father immediately stood up and volunteered the services of him and his son. The woman thanked him profusely before venturing back into the maelstrom, to return to her sick husband.

"Let's go, Fred," Cherrill's father said, handing him a coat. Frederick, always up for some excitement, eagerly followed his father into the merciless night. The cobblestones were slick beneath their feet, as wind and rain whipped and stung their faces. The two came to the little stone bridge that crossed the Thames, a wide, angry serpent of churning black and moon-white foam that thundered loudly as it passed under their feet. They turned left at the end of the bridge and trudged past Overy Manor House, eventually coming to the quaint miller's home. There, they got a key to the mill from the miller's wife and proceeded with their task.

The mill was only several yards from the house and greeted the two Cherrills with a creepy symphony of groans and creeks. It was almost like something out of a Sexton Blake serial, the young Cherrill thought as the wind tore through the ancient structure, slamming unseen boards and doors. In these conditions, he could easily imagine the mill as a living, breathing creature made of stone. It writhed and moaned around them as the storm beat at its ancient skin. Cherrill's father pulled a book of matches from one of his pockets and lit several of the old lanterns fastened to the wall. In the pallid glow, a mountain of corn—bundled in canvas sacks—presented itself to father and son. The corn had to be ground into coarse meal so that farmers would have something to feed their cattle. Cherrill's father opened the mill's sluice, while the boy began dragging sacks to the hopper. Outside, the angry waters of the Thames throttled the mill wheel and brought the ancient machinery inside to life.

After opening the sluice, Cherrill's father set the grinding stones in place. Now father and son fed the corn into the sluice. The labor soon had the two of them wiping sweat from their brows and breathing heavily. The chute discharged the warm meal into canvas sacks below. The smell reminded the young Cherrill of the local bakery when fresh bread was pulled from the oven. As rain continued to beat the windows outside and wind fluttered the flames on the wall-mounted lanterns, the father-and-son team worked in silence. The mill wheel creaked in protest as the angry river slammed into the wooden paddles and turned the large contraption ever faster. Through the water-smeared window, young Cherrill could just see the dark shape of the wheel turning on its great axle. He wondered how much more of the river's punishment it would take before the whole mechanism came apart and crashed into the raging torrent of water that roared under the floorboards on which he and his father stood.

At long last, after much sweat and toil, the work was completed. Lingering clouds of white dust parched their throats and settled on sweat-soaked skin. Cherrill's father went into the wheelhouse and shut off the sluice. Outside, the great wheel slowed to an eventual halt, until all that moved were the strands of weeds that dangled from the warped paddles. The older Cherrill walked back into the mill and opened a trapdoor in the floor, revealing a well. He knew the wheel's frenzied activity had probably stirred up the eels bedding on the river's muddy bottom. From the wall he retrieved an eel spear secured by two metal hooks. He returned to the edge of the trapdoor and gave his son a conspiratorial glance. In one fluid motion, he brought his arm back and plunged the spear's pointed tip into the dark water below the trapdoor's edge. He brought the spear tip back up with a quick jerking motion and flung a fat, writhing eel onto the dusty wood floor. He ordered his awestruck son to grab it and put it in an empty corn sack.

The young boy rolled and wrestled with the eel, trying to get a firm grip on the slick skin. It was a frustrating endeavor, but one the lad thoroughly enjoyed, and he laughed as he thrust the slippery creature into a sack. The boy's father flung several more up onto the floor. The father's task was easier than his son's, for a steel grating at the bottom of the well trapped the eels as the currents swept them downstream. Wrestling with the eels and stuffing them in the sack was almost as tiring as grinding the corn. The thought of the eels frying on the stovetop back home, however, made it all worthwhile. Eventually, Cherrill's father returned the eel spear to the hooks on the wall and cheerfully slapped his son on the shoulder. Young Frederick laughed, then grimaced when he looked at his hands. Eel slime covered his palms, and it clung to his fingers in mucuslike strands. He held his hands out in front of him as though they were foreign objects that disgusted him. What he wanted to do was wipe them on something and remove the sticky film that made his palms glisten.

The amusement derived from their eel hunt had momentarily distracted their attention from the ferocity of the weather outside. Now nature reasserted itself. A huge gust of wind slammed into the mill, causing the building to sway violently. The mill's oak-beam supports screamed, and an ominous grinding sound reached out to them from the stone foundations. There was a whip-crack against the window as a torrent of rain slapped the side of the old structure and drummed heavily on the roof. Young Cherrill was startled off balance. With the writhing sack of eels in one hand, he reached out with his other hand to grab something. His fingers made contact with the grain chute, its surface polished from years of use. From the beams above, a steady downpour of dirt and meal dust covered the two Cherrills. Then all was quiet. The wind died down, the rainfall softened, and the mill once again seemed solid on its foundations.

When Cherrill removed his hand from the chute, he was stunned at what he saw. The dust and grain meal that had rained down from the support beams had adhered itself to the slime Cherrill's hand had left on the chute. And there, in the dim flicker of the lanterns on the wall, were Frederick Cherrill's fingerprints. Behind him, Cherrill's father was talking, but the words fell on deaf ears. The sight before him completely mesmerized the young boy. He absentmindedly pushed past his father and grabbed one of the lanterns from the wall. Holding the flame up to the chute, he moved in for a closer look. His breath came and went as though he had just run a race. Upon exhaling, he blew clear some of the excess dust on the chute, which revealed the prints in even more startling clarity. Cherrill's father came closer to see what had grabbed his son's attention with such an unwavering grip.

"My fingerprints," Cherrill said, pointing at the chute.

His father nodded and, like his son, leaned in for a closer look. The two of them shared a boyish fondness for the adventures of Sexton Blake, and now they shared a fascination with the intricate patterns of swirls and loops so evident on the chute. Cherrill's father slapped his son on the back and said perhaps the prints were an omen of things to come—such as the adventurous life of a great detective, one that would even rival the creation of Sir Arthur Conan Doyle. The boy smiled at his father, for the idea greatly appealed to him. After a moment of silent pondering, the elder Cherrill said it was time to go. The two of them put on their coats, grabbed the sack of eels and readied themselves for the cold outside.

Night still hung heavy over the village, obscuring the large tree the monks had planted outside the mill centuries before. Mercifully, the storm had weakened somewhat. The two walked along the shiny cobblestones to the miller's house. They knocked on the door and told him the good news: The mountain of corn had been ground to meal. The miller expressed his gratitude and was even more pleased when the young boy handed him an eel to fry up for the next evening's dinner. With that, the Cherrills bid the miller and his wife a good night and proceeded home.

In his room, young Cherrill crawled into bed and pulled the sheets up under his chin. Through the curtains drawn across the window, he could see the silhouettes of naked tree branches stirring in the wind. He had heard stories that the ghosts of ancient monks haunted the old mill, roaming its grounds in shades of spectral gray, their faces concealed by the low-hanging hoods of their cowls. His mind now dwelled on this unearthly image, as the wind blew about the house. He thought of the eels that he and his father had technically poached. It was hardly a crime, but he couldn't help but think that those ghostly monks were now onto him, for had he not left a clue as to his identity? In the fog of his increasingly sleepy mind, the swirling patterns of those fingerprints came back to him—and standing at the chute, examining the trace evidence he had left behind, was the ethereal mist of a phantom monk.

Cherrill eventually left Dorchester for Oxford, with the plan to study art and perhaps learn the craft of woodcarving, but a mishap of biology set him on a different course. In the midst of his studies, he was sidelined by a cervical rib—a protrusion of bone extending from the seventh cervical vertebra, near the neck, that can push against a nerve or an artery, causing severe discomfort. He was admitted to the hospital for surgery and, during his recovery, shared his room with a former officer of the Metropolitan Police Department. The one-time copper explained to the enthralled

Cherrill that he had been shot in the face some time back while trying to apprehend a suspect. The resulting injuries required regular visits to the hospital for surgery to preserve the sight in his right eye.

A fascinated Cherrill grilled the man about his experiences on the force. While they bore little semblance to the escapades of Sexton Blake, they were nevertheless captivating and set Cherrill's mind to exploring the possibilities of a career with Scotland Yard. The policeman told Cherrill that the commissioner he had served under—Sir Edward Henry—was something of a revolutionary in the burgeoning field of fingerprints and had written a book titled *The Classification and Uses of Fingerprints.* Cherrill sent a friend to the local library to find a copy of the book and bring it to him in the hospital. From the first page, every word seized Cherrill's attention, and when he had finished, he knew what he wanted to do with his life.

In 1914, Frederick Cherrill joined the London Metropolitan Police Force as Police Constable Cherrill, 1211 V, and was assigned to Wandsworth Common Police Station. Cherrill endured the monotony of walking the beat for six years, investigating petty crimes and learning how to carry himself on the stand while presenting evidence in court. Although now a man, Cherrill's mind still harkened back to the grand adventures of Sexton Blake and the supervillains who pitted themselves against him. He was eager to test his mental prowess and employ detecting skills against a worthy adversary. London's police force had faced off against a long, distinguished gallery of rogues since its inception. From Jack the Ripper to Dr. Crippen, the department's case files boasted names of criminals that still enthralled the public. And for every evil mastermind, there was the detective who tackled the case. Cherrill believed it would not be long before he, too, faced off against an opponent of note.

Although he found the job of constable somewhat lacking in mental stimulation, Cherrill's time on the beat opened him up to a whole new world of knowledge. Beating the pavement, he would make note of used bookstores that caught his fancy and—at the earliest possible opportunity—would take the time to explore the yellowed and dusty treasures on the cluttered shelves within. Cherrill's interests extended far beyond police work and the art of detection. He tore through books on art and history, and took it upon himself to learn about botany. It was not long before his bookshelf at home became as cluttered as some of those in the used bookstores he frequented. Cherrill considered reading to be an important part of police work, for he believed every branch of knowledge was beneficial to a detective. Investigators, he maintained, should be walking encyclopedias.

Cherrill's sense of humor and artistic skills made him popular with his fellow constables and senior officers. His love of art never abandoned him, and he made a point of taking pencil and paints to paper whenever he had the chance. In London, there was no shortage of artistic inspiration—but some of Cherrill's favorite subjects were the very people he worked with. Cherrill's fellow police officers soon found themselves on the receiving end of his drawing pencil. Generally, the finished product was not what one might consider a flattering portrait. No, Cherrill's drawings had a tendency to play upon the more pronounced physical characteristics of his subjects. A senior officer secretly known about the police station for a rather large nose was likely to wind up in Cherrill's sketchpad boasting a profile not unlike Pinnochio's. A constable with big ears might end up being portrayed on paper as some helpless soul with two large, winglike appendages on the sides of his head. Despite these somewhat questionable depictions, Cherrill never kept his portraits secret. He freely shared them with his subjects, who—for the most part—accepted them with good grace and more often than not asked the artist to sign them. From time to time, however, a less-than-flattered sergeant or other commanding officer had a few choice words for the young man.

Cherrill's years as a constable were not completely void of action. On the night of November 24, 1915, he experienced the excitement he so desperately sought, while patrolling a street normally bustling with people. On this specific night, however, few souls were about. The lack of pedestrian activity meant that Police Constable Cherrill was the first person to see flames coming through the windows of a flat above a nearby shop. Over the roar of the fire and the sound of breaking glass, Cherrill could hear a woman screaming. He ran to the storefront and entered the premises, working his way to the back, where the stairs were located. The heat from the fire radiated through the stairwell door, from under which thin wisps of smoke curled around Cherrill's ankles.

He paused briefly to ponder the situation, only to be spurred back into action by the woman's screams coming from above. A great wave of heat swept over him when he opened the door, forcing him to raise his arms to his face. His efforts to climb the stairs were repeatedly thwarted by flame and smoke. His lungs burning and his eyes watering, he ran outside and went to the shop next door, where he borrowed a small stepladder. His plan was to climb the ladder and enter the burning building through a second-floor window. Unfortunately, the ladder was too short for the task.

The situation grew increasingly dire. The flames devoured more of the shop, and the woman's screams became more frantic. Cherrill called to her, trying to reassure her as he desperately looked around for something that might assist his cause. At that moment, a window cleaner just happened to come sauntering down the street. Without even asking him, Cherrill snatched away the cleaner's ladder. He slapped it against the side of the building, climbed up and scrambled through one of the windows.

Thick smoke clouded the room he entered. The walls and ceiling burned violently in shades of orange and yellow. Hot, acrid air filled his lungs with each inward breath, and stung his eyes and singed his nose. He wiped the sweat from his brow and, using one arm to shield his face from the heat and the other to feel in front of him, made his way across the room. The situation in the hallway was just as desperate. Flames climbed the walls and traversed the ceiling. The floor felt hot beneath Cherrill's feet as he made his way down the hallway and opened the various doors that branched off it. In each room, furnishings burned. Paintings were melting on the walls and rugs smoldered on the floor. Flames danced across chairs and devoured tables— and all the while, the unseen woman kept screaming. In the last room, Cherrill found his damsel in distress sprawled on the floor and, in his words, "almost senseless."

He scooped the woman up and hoisted her over his shoulders, a task not made easy by the near suffocating conditions. His back bent under the heavy burden, Cherrill staggered back down the hallway to the room he had first entered. He was relieved to find the ladder still in place at the window and—much to his surprise—was able to maneuver the rungs down to street level without dropping the cumbersome load slung across his shoulders. He carefully laid the woman down on the pavement and checked her pulse. Her eyes flew open as he did this and she sat bolt upright. She grabbed the collar of Cherrill's uniform and screamed, "What about Nellie?"

By now a rather large crowd had gathered in front of the burning building. The woman's desperate inquiry drew a startled gasp from the enthralled audience, prompting one of them to shout, "There's a kid in one of the bedrooms!" Cherrill knew exactly what he had to do. Again, he mounted the ladder and climbed up to the window, through which poured thick columns of black smoke. Surely, Cherrill thought, no child could survive conditions such as these! His skin began to burn as he fought his way again through the hellish conditions. In the hallway, he feared his face, hands and forehead were on the verge of blistering. His uniform felt hot against his skin, and he worried the material might soon burst into flame, or that his shoes might scald his feet. Sweat stung eyes already red and raw from the smoke.

He tried calling the child's name, but he couldn't muster enough air to yell; cough violently is all he did. The walls in the hallway writhed in a fiery display, and the floor creaked in protest beneath his feet. Cherrill's mind grimly pondered the worst-case scenario as the world disintegrated around him. He couldn't imagine how he'd bring himself to tell the woman her daughter was dead. Cherrill half-expected to find a small child lying in a crumpled heap on the floor, but the fear never came to pass. He continued his frantic search until he found himself succumbing to the heat and smoke. His head began to swoon. His thoughts were losing their sense of cohesiveness. In a semi-daze, he fought his way back to the window through which he had entered and its waiting ladder.

He rubbed the back of one smoke-smeared hand across his watering eyes and blinked hard. His vision wavered, and the world around him presented itself in triplicate. Sapped of nearly all his physical strength, Cherrill couldn't maintain a tight grasp on the ladder's rungs. Momentarily afraid to move, out of fear of falling, he was forced downward by a burst of flame from the window. He descended the ladder, struggling to keep his balance, but lost his footing halfway down and hit the pavement on his back. He landed with a bruising thud and made one slight effort to get up before losing consciousness. How long he was out, he never knew for sure, but with consciousness came the news that Nellie had escaped harm. When Cherrill asked to see her, he was most unhappy to discover that what he thought was the woman's child was actually her pet dog, who had found a way out of the burning building unassisted.

Cherrill's daring exploits did not go unnoticed. From the Society of Protection of Life from Fire, the young police constable received a medal and a check for two guineas. Shortly thereafter, the very opportunity Cherrill had longed for came his way. In 1920, a vacancy opened in Scotland Yard's Criminal Investigation Department. At the same time, a position became available in the Fingerprint Department. Cherrill wasted little time in deciding which opening he would pursue. His childhood experience at the old mill that stormy night seemed a lifetime ago, but the memory of it and the thrill of seeing the swirls and loops of his fingerprints on the grain chute had remained a strong constant. Cherrill had taken it upon himself over the years to become well versed in the history of fingerprints. Much of his knowledge came from Sir Edward Henry's book, *The Classification and Uses of Fingerprints,* which he had read in the hospital while recuperating from his operation. The complexity of fingerprints and the evolution of fingerprinting as a tool to fight crime appealed to Cherrill's fascination with science. The aesthetics of prints pleased the artist in him.

Sir Edward Henry—before becoming a knight of the realm—was merely Edward Henry, inspector general of police in one of the Empire's far-flung corners—Bengal, to be precise. A man of advanced thought, Henry believed that fingerprints could be used in the identification of suspects and the solving of crimes. At the time, the primary method of criminal identification was the Bertillon system. Devised by French criminologist Alphonse Bertillon, the system was based on skeletal measurements and other characteristics of the human body, such as the width of the head, the span of one's arms and the length of one's fingers. Adopted by authorities in France in the 1880s, the system soon gained acceptance in countries around the world. It reached Edward Henry's corner of the globe in 1892. Bertillon's system, however, was prone to inaccuracies and burdened by limitations. The first problem lay in the taking of the measurements themselves. One officer—in measuring certain physical traits of a criminal—might apply more or less pressure on the calipers than another officer, thus producing two different sets of measurements that failed to match upon comparison. Another problem could be found in the system's reliance on the physical traits of the adult body. Most criminals began committing their acts before they'd stopped growing, hence measurements taken earlier in life might not be the same as measurements taken later. Finally, one had to capture a criminal first before his physical traits could be cataloged, measured and recorded under the system's 243 basic categories.

Henry found Bertillon's approach cumbersome and increasingly obsolete. He believed fingerprinting to be the identification system of the future. The British had been making use of fingerprints since 1858, when Sir William Herschel—chief magistrate of the Hooghly District in Jungipoor, India—began requiring members of the local populace to sign official documents with the prints of their right middle and index fingers. This was merely done to enforce the binding nature of various contracts and letters, for many natives could not sign their names. Consequently, Herschel soon found himself fascinated by what he perceived to be the distinguishing characteristics of fingerprints. He was not a man of scientific training, and his knowledge of biology was scant. What Herschel learned in this new field was through his own casual observations. As his collection of fingerprinted documents grew, so too did his interest in the complex pattern of prints and their potential as a method of identification. Examining numerous impressions through a magnifying glass, Herschel noticed that no two prints ever appeared to be the same and that none changed over the course of a person's lifetime. It seemed to Herschel that such information could be useful in helping to identify criminals, and he approached his superiors with the idea. Unfortunately, his superiors lacked foresight and expressed little interest in his theories.

Like Herschel, Henry sought to create a system for fingerprints that would allow authorities to categorize and compare prints of suspected criminals. Henry wanted his system to be independent of Bertillon's, the latter still being widely used despite its apparent problems. Henry eventually succeeded in creating a complex classification system for fingerprints based on numeric values. Each finger was assigned a certain value, thus allowing prints to be broken down into 1,024 primary groupings. These groupings were then subdivided into further groupings based on the physical characteristics of individual prints. The system went into effect in Bengal in 1897 and met with instant success. Highly encouraged, Henry approached the Indian government and asked them to officially compare his fingerprinting system to the Bertillon method of identification. The government—intrigued by Henry's work—set up an independent committee to compare his system with Bertillon's. The committee met in March 1897 and quickly found fingerprinting to be more reliable in every way over anthropometric measurements. Thus, in June 1897, the governor general signed his name to a resolution adopting the use of fingerprinting over the Bertillon system in British India. The French method of identification would soon be rendered useless.

In London, word of Henry's work in India caught the interest of Scotland Yard. The Metropolitan Police Department in 1900 scrapped the Bertillon method in favor of Henry's. In May the following year, Henry was recalled from India to become the Yard's assistant commissioner of the Criminal Investigation Department. In this capacity he set about the task of creating the Fingerprint Department, for which Frederick Cherrill would eventually work. Henry selected the bureau's men himself and trained them in the intricacies of his new science.

C. H. Stedman worked as the bureau's first chief, succeeded by Charles Stockley Collins in 1908. It was under Collins that Cherrill first worked when he passed his entrance exam and joined the bureau in 1920. Even after attaining the job he so desperately sought, Cherrill refused to rest on his laurels. Like the criminal mind, fingerprinting was a constantly evolving entity. Cherrill made sure he kept abreast of the latest breakthroughs, spending hours studying, combing the Yard's increasing catalog of prints and reviewing the different characteristics of each finger. As Cherrill would write years later in his memoirs: "The fingerprint expert must be able to state that he has personally examined thousands of prints taken from different fingers, and has made an exhaustive study of the unique markings which Nature has placed on each individual finger."

Although Cherrill took great pleasure in his work, he had brought his crosshairs to bear on the top job. He worked for the next eighteen years under three chiefs and did his utmost to learn all he could from each one. In 1938, when Superintendent Harry Battley retired as the bureau's head, Cherrill finally got the big office. Although a man of good humor, he took his new position seriously and understood the immense responsibility with which he had now been burdened. He was the Yard's foremost expert on fingerprints, meaning he would be called to testify at trials where a defendant's life depended on the evidence he presented. There was no room for doubt or questionable knowledge. His understanding of a print's complexity had to be absolute. In court, when he said a particular finger left a particular print, he knew the magistrates and jury would take his word on the subject as gospel.

Even on cases of a less spectacular nature, Cherrill thrilled at the prospect of hunting for prints. The ingenuity of nature never ceased to enrapture him. The characteristics of prints were almost too complex to be considered just some random aspect of creation, like the color of one's eyes or hair. There was something too deliberate in the intricate patterns. The Yard's reputation for print identification was unequaled. The bureau remained busy—even when no immediate cases were at hand—assisting other agencies with their investigations. It's what maintained Cherrill's interest in the job—but there was more to it than that. Working for the Yard meant he had ingratiated himself into the annals of history. It was an honor for a man who harbored such a keen sense of the past.

Scotland Yard came in to existence in 1829. Crime prevention—not detection—was the primary focus of the new department, created by Sir Robert Peel, home secretary and leader of the House of Commons. The fact that the force would answer directly to Peel at the Home Office endowed officers with the lasting nicknames of "bobbies" and "peelers." The evolution of London's police force was a dark and violent one. Although considered the world's center of power, the British capital was a cluttered and dirty metropolis rife with crime and unsavory characters.

The first semblance of a police department in London was the unlikely work of Henry Fielding, a novelist and playwright best known for his work *The History of Tom Jones,* released in 1749—a year after he became London's chief magistrate. Something of a cad, Fielding was a rumored drunkard and one who took great pleasure in the company of women. Many considered him a good-time boy and hopeless with money, but he possessed a sharp intellect and his wit could sting. In the late 1730s, Fielding—already known for his literary endeavors—moved to London from the rural haven of Dorset after his spendthrift ways bankrupted him and his wife, Charlotte. He took up position as manager and chief playwright of the Little Theatre in the Haymarket. He had already secured a favorable reputation with his 1731 play *The Tragedy of Tragedies; or,*

The Life and Death of Tom Thumb the Great, a lampoon of other theatrical works that took themselves far too seriously.

Unfortunately for Fielding, his wit proved to be too much for the establishment. The Licensing Act of 1737, which declared that only plays approved by the government could take to the stage, unceremoniously ended Fielding's theater career. The law itself was the result of Fielding's own work, which savaged various government policies of the day and depicted local officials as corrupt and scheming. For a man who took great pleasure in publicizing his opinion, there remained only one other career to pursue. With the theater no longer a viable outlet to voice his frustrations, Fielding took up journalism and became the editor of *The Champion* in 1739. He adopted the not-so-subtle pseudonym Captain Hercules Vinegar and penned a number of highly acidic editorials blasting the policies of Prime Minister Robert Walpole's government. All the while, he maintained a somewhat dubious reputation as a wild man, drinking heavily and spending beyond his means.

Despite his outwardly carefree attitude toward life, his existence was a grim one. Although only in his early thirties, Fielding's hard living had taken a toll on his health. His wife, Charlotte—whom he married in 1734 at the age of twenty-seven—also suffered from various maladies, but the two continued to struggle on. There was little else they could do, for they had two children to raise. Fielding continued in his capacity as editor of *The Champion* until leaving the newspaper business in 1741 to focus on his creative writing. In 1742, he published his comic novel *Joseph Andrews*. The following year saw the release of *Jonathan Wild*, the fictionalized biography of one of Britain's more colorful criminals. The death of his daughter and his wife's deteriorating health, however, marred the success of these books. Charlotte finally succumbed to her illnesses in 1744 in Bath. Devastated by his wife's passing, Fielding turned his amorous attention to Charlotte's former maid, Mary Daniel. Shunning the social snobbery of the times, he married Mary—who was six months pregnant with his son—in 1747.

Fielding by now had decided to put his knowledge of the law to use and—through the intervention of powerful acquaintances—became the justice of the peace for Westminster and Middlesex in 1748, having been admitted to the bar eight years prior. With his newfound authority came an end to his financial worries and a deeper level of social awareness. He maintained an office at No. 4 Bow Street, where—in 1740—Sir Thomas de Veil had established a courthouse near Covent Garden. It was through his daily contact with the city's criminal element that Fielding set in motion Scotland Yard's evolution. Fielding's work as a magistrate only enlarged his already well-known public persona. He channeled his energies into stamping out street crime and ending mob violence. To achieve these ends, in 1750 Fielding organized the Bow Street Runners, a small constabulary force of eight honest men, out of which Scotland Yard would eventually emerge. The Runners—initially known as Robin Redbreasts and Raw Lobsters because of the bright scarlet waistcoats they wore—quickly earned a reputation on London's rough-and-tumble streets. They served writs, arrested criminals and performed detective work. Their duties and the effort they put forward were a far cry from the law enforcers who'd preceded them. In the years leading up to the Runners, the night watchman's job was to patrol the streets from 10 p.m. until sunrise, walking London's cluttered cobblestone thoroughfares and dank alleys in search of criminal activity. They were expected to confront all suspicious characters they came across. And suspicious characters ran rampant in London. During the day, law enforcement fell to the beadles, full-time officials tasked with maintaining order on the streets and organizing the night watch in their sections of the city. These early efforts, however, suffered from a lack of coordination and decentralized control.

A more dubious form of crime fighter was the thief taker, an individual who worked both sides of the law. The 1697 Act of Parliament offered rewards for the apprehension of serious criminals, such as murderers and highwaymen. Newspapers in the early eighteenth century also began to publicize rewards for those who brought nefarious individuals to justice. The offering of so much money gave rise to a mercenary sort of character, for thief takers were hardly honest citizens. The majority of them had a working knowledge of London's underworld, generally the result of their participation in less-than-savory activities. They worked in a world of shadows, serving as middlemen between criminals and those trying to bring them to justice. They worked with the victims of crimes to negotiate fees wrongdoers could pay as restitution for stealing goods. Additionally, they served as informants and snitched to the authorities in exchange for hefty rewards. Such activity invariably bred a corrupt streak in many men—one of whom was Jonathan Wild, "Thief-taker General of England and Ireland." It was the same Jonathan Wild—considered to be Great Britain's first crime lord—who inspired Henry Fielding's popular story of the same name.

Wild worked with authorities to stamp out London's underworld. His cooperation with the powers-that-be resulted in the jailing and hanging of countless criminals. But Wild's actions were not as altruistic as they seemed. While he was busy pointing fingers and whispering in ears, Wild busied himself masterminding his own unlawful endeavors. A buckle-maker by trade, Wild's first encounter with the underside of humanity came in his early twenties when he was tossed into a debtors' prison in London. He served a two- to four-year sentence, during which he fraternized with a number of individuals who boasted skills one would be hard-pressed to find in the everyday workforce. The stories told by pickpockets, burglars and prostitutes enthralled Wild and played upon his sense of adventure. Their lives were certainly more interesting than that of a buckle-maker!

While in prison, Wild met Mary Milliner, a prostitute. He already had a wife and child in Wolverhampton, but he abandoned them to start a new life in the capital and took Mary as his mistress. When the two of them were eventually released, they moved into a house in Covent Garden. Mary immediately returned to her old ways. She sold her sex and entertained customers in pungent alleyways. While the men were busy thrusting themselves into his lady, Wild snuck up behind them and took them for all they had. The couple's criminal activity lined their pockets with enough money to enable them to purchase a pub called the King's Head. Not only was the establishment one where thirsty souls could down a pint of ale, it was a crook's haven where thieves could sell the goods they pilfered for a tidy profit. The man who generally purchased the stolen property was none other than Wild. He soon realized he could use his dealings with the underworld to further his economic advancement.

He opened—when one really boiled it down to its most

basic essence—a lost-and-found business. People came to him with descriptions of items that had recently been stolen from them. Wild sat and listened to their tales with a look of concern and understanding painted across his face. In soothing tones he would tell them not to worry; he would do his utmost to track the stolen property down and return it to where it rightfully belonged. What Wild's clients failed to realize was that in most cases, he already possessed the goods they so desperately sought. Most of the time, he had already purchased the missing items from the fencers who frequented the King's Head. For his clients, he would go through the motions and pretend to hit the streets in search of their stolen valuables. When he "found" them, he charged them a finder's fee before handing the property over. He quickly took his scheme to the next level. Leaning over the crowded bar at the King's Head, Wild began paying his clientele to target victims and steal items of great sentimental value. The thieves would be paid for their service. Invariably, the target of the scam would eventually make his or her way to Wild's office in Newtoner's Lane and explain their upsetting circumstance. Wild would listen to the story of woe and promise to do his utmost. When Wild eventually "recovered" the missing goods, the client would be so overcome with joy there was no price he or she wouldn't pay to have it back.

Wild soon took his operation citywide, and the money began to flow in rapidly. All the while, he worked with authorities to jail criminals who failed to operate within the confines of his burgeoning empire. On one occasion, a tip he provided resulted in the arrests of more than a hundred street robbers. He became a hero to the public and an invaluable asset to the criminal justice system. Authorities failed to realize that the man helping them also owned warehouses filled wall-to-wall and floor-to-ceiling with stolen property. Wild's operation had by now gone international. He had acquired a sloop that took goods to and from Holland, and smuggled brandy and fine linens into London in the process. Life for Jonathan Wild was good. But, as is life, all good things eventually came to an end. Wild failed to keep in mind that criminals are not the most loyal business compatriots, for they look out only for themselves. It proved to be a lesson in which Wild was educated the hard way, and one that would cost him his life.

Two of Wild's minions—one of whom was the captain of his sloop—were eventually arrested for their shady activities. One of the men turned Wild in by telling authorities of his secret warehouses, which were promptly searched and all the property within seized. Wild was arrested and the extent of his criminal empire came to light. The public, which at one point had adored the suave and charismatic thief taker, quickly turned against him and demanded he be stretched by the neck. The public got its wish. Wild was tried, convicted and sentenced to death. The day of reckoning came on May 25, 1725. In a desperate attempt to cheat the hangman, Wild gulped down a vile of poison in his jail cell just hours before he was scheduled to mount the scaffold. Much to his chagrin, the toxin failed to do the job, and he was held to answer for his crimes. The trip to the scaffold was a brutal affair, as a crowd of thousands had gathered for the spectacle and took great delight in pelting Wild with whatever they could get their hands on.

The crooked exploits of Jonathan Wild all but exposed the shortcomings of the thief takers, yet their services were still utilized by authorities because of their underworld contacts. But by the mid-1700s, Fielding's small force of constables had made a name for itself. While the Bow

Street Runners waged their street-level war against crime and thuggery, Fielding tackled the same issues with his pen, writing "An Inquiry into the Causes of the Late Increase of Robbers." In it, he argued too many people were flooding into London expecting to find the easy life. Crime, he wrote, was becoming the alternative for those who didn't want to work for a living. His opinions were highly respected and even garnered the support of the government, unlike his plays years earlier.

By 1750, Fielding's younger half brother, John, had joined him at No. 4 Bow Street as his assistant. Despite being blinded in a navy accident when he was nineteen, John Fielding excelled in his study of law and was a notable social reformer. Together, the Fieldings pursued the concept of deterrence, hoping the fear of being caught would prevent criminals from perpetrating acts of violence and other misdeeds. They gathered information on known criminals and distributed it among the public, which eventually led to the publication of the *Police Gazette,* an illustrated rag carrying news of city crime. They further evolved the concept of thief takers by bringing them under the direct control of the magistrates, who now dispatched them with the specific task of hunting culprits down. Through their efforts, the Fieldings were soon overseeing a vast intelligence network at their Bow Street office that funneled all sorts of information from the underworld.

Henry Fielding's bad health finally got the better of him, and he died in 1754. John Fielding was appointed magistrate at Bow Street in his place. He advanced the work started by his brother and first used the word "police" in the manner it's now used today. Dubbed "The Blind Beak of Bow Street," it was believed he could recognize more than three thousand criminals merely by the sound of their voices. Fielding believed the only effective way to fight crime lay in the creation of an organized police force. To keep tabs on the city's darker goings-on, he organized a record-keeping system, which eventually became the Criminal Records Office. He believed in the rehabilitation of youthful offenders and offered them a second chance at life by enlisting them in the Royal Navy. In the early 1760s, the government heeded Fielding's calls for an organized police department and hired ten mounted officers to patrol the outskirts of the city. Although successful, the patrols eventually fell victim to a shortfall in government funding. Nevertheless, Fielding continued his efforts to further the fight against crime. He asked the public to report crimes and believed in publicizing the successful apprehension of criminals.

Despite the advances made in law enforcement under the Fielding brothers, London went without the police department it needed until 1829. That year, Home Secretary Robert Peel put before Parliament his Metropolitan Police Act, resulting in the creation of a centralized police force directly under Peel's control. The initial structure of the department, as outlined by Peel, included eight superintendents, twenty inspectors, eighty-eight sergeants and nearly four hundred constables. Paid a salary of three shillings a day, uniformed constables armed with truncheons were assigned specific beats, the idea being that a high police profile on the streets would scare any nefarious thoughts out of the heads of would-be wrongdoers. Dressed in top hat and tailcoat, the first officers took to London's streets on September 25,1829. As with any new organization, there were growing pains. In the first six months, thirty-two hundred men were recruited into the

department. Of these, roughly sixteen hundred were
quickly dismissed for drinking on the job or simply failing
to show up for work. The department established headquarters at 4 Whitehall Place, the back entrance of which
opened onto Great Scotland Yard, believed to be so named
because it served as a former site for visiting Scottish kings
before the union of England and Scotland. The name Scotland Yard soon attached itself to the police force. The dangers of patrolling the streets of London were immediately
apparent. Within a year of Scotland Yard's creation, two
police constables had been killed in the line of duty. Joseph
Grantham died after being kicked in the head while trying
to make an arrest during a riot. John Lang was stabbed to
death one night after confronting three thieves in Gray's
Inn Lane.

In August 1842, Scotland Yard established its Detective
Branch. In those early days of homicide investigation, detectives responding to a scene were forced to handle evidence
with their bare hands. Clues found near a body—whether it
be a bloody knife, a torn piece of clothing or human hair—
were collected by finger and wrapped in a piece of paper or
deposited in an envelope for safekeeping. Forensic science
being what it was in those days, police had no way of knowing how the improper handling of evidence compromised its
quality. Such methods continued until 1924, when the Yard
introduced its "murder bag" in the wake of a particularly
gruesome killing.

The crime scene was a seaside bungalow in Eastbourne.
What detectives found in the four-bedroom home following
a phoned-in tip was horrific even by the most brutal standards. Before detectives even entered the house, they could
smell something foul drifting from it on the salty ocean
breeze. Aside from the bedrooms, there was a sitting room,

a kitchen and a scullery. The violence that had occurred within the house left no room untouched. A thick trail of blood ran from the sitting room. It crossed the hallway and passed through a bedroom into the scullery, where boiled human remains were found in a saucepan and a tub. Detectives discovered a blood-smeared saw in one bedroom, while fragments of torched bone littered the fireplaces in the sitting and dining rooms. Blood on the lid of a biscuit tin found in the kitchen drew the attention of one detective. Opening it revealed a heart and other internal organs crammed inside. In another room, investigators came across a large trunk from which the awful stench that permeated the place seemed to originate. Prying open the lid, detectives found a woman's dismembered body.

Sir Bernard Spilsbury responded to the scene to help search for missing body parts. When the pathologist entered the bungalow, he was horrified to find one detective using his bare hands to scoop up mounds of rotting flesh and deposit them in a bucket. Spilsbury gave the detective a quick dissertation on the health hazards associated with such an activity and asked the policeman why he wasn't wearing rubber gloves. The detective gave Spilsbury a puzzled look and told him he never wore rubber gloves. Since the Murder Squad's creation seventeen years prior, this was how things had been done. Spilsbury made a note to bring this up with the proper authorities back at the Yard. He then began his own crime-scene examination. Over the course of the day, Spilsbury and detectives retrieved more than one thousand pieces of bone fragments in the bungalow's fireplaces. The stench of decomposing flesh in the residence was so strong that Spilsbury set his workstation up outside. The woman's body had to be pieced back together like a jigsaw puzzle. An autopsy eventually revealed that the victim—later identified as thirty-four-year-old Emily Kaye—was three months pregnant when she was hacked to death. Spilsbury would later admit that the barbarity of the crime and the condition of the victim made the Kaye murder one his most disturbing cases.

Kaye's killer—Patrick Mahon, a married man who had an affair with Kaye and panicked when he learned she was pregnant—rendezvoused with the hangman for the killing. In the wake of the case, Spilsbury met with Detective Superintendent William Brown—chief of the Murder Squad—and shared his concerns regarding detectives handling human remains with their naked hands. Brown and Spilsbury's consultation resulted in the murder bag, a kit that was to be carried by all detectives responding to a homicide. In the bag were rubber gloves, tweezers, containers for evidence, a magnifying glass, swabs and other items useful for the collection of evidence. Over the years, the murder bag's contents would evolve with the advancement of investigative techniques and forensic methods.

In 1890—two years after Jack the Ripper's East End rampage—Scotland Yard moved its headquarters to the Victoria Embankment and took up residence in the red-and-white gothic building it would call home through both world wars. From blackouts to zeppelin raids, flying bombs and parachute mines, the war years brought a new element of danger to police work that claimed the lives of thirty-two officers in London during the 1914–1918 conflict. When war again fell upon the city two decades later, the toll on Scotland Yard increased. Air raids and the dangers of patrolling streets in the pitch black cost the Metropolitan Police Department more than one hundred men. One bomb in 1940 wiped out a dozen constables; another took out six when it slammed into a West End police station. But amid all this chaos, the Yard continued to tackle acts of common criminality and the more sinister deeds of darkness borne of the blackout and wartime desperation.

FEBRUARY 11, 1942

SIX

Evelyn Oatley's body still lay in the morgue. The gaping wounds were stitched, and her body had been cleansed of the dried blood that formed a crust on her pale skin. Her husband came to London by train, traveling down from Blackpool to identify her. Despite the emotional and geographical distance between them, word of Evelyn's death left Harry Oatley feeling shocked and bereaved. He could offer no suggestions when questioned by authorities as to who could have done such a thing. A gentle person, Evelyn maintained—despite her occupation—a childlike sense of wonder for things, he said. She fought against the jadedness inherent in her work and struggled to hold on to the belief that something better would eventually come her way. She tried to seek out meaningful partners in her quest for optimism, though she couldn't help but let her own self-doubts about love and human nature dim her view of relationships. Harry knew Evelyn occasionally dated a

Canadian soldier. He had met the man on one occasion and found him, considering the circumstances, to be quite personable. No, he was at a loss as to how gentle Evelyn met her gruesome end.

At the Westminster Mortuary Harry stood in silence, the battle to keep his emotions under control played out on his face. Inspector Charles Gray lingered in the background as the mortuary assistant wheeled the iron gurney out of the cold storage room. The assistant looked at Gray, who gave a subtle nod. The white sheet was pulled down to just above the breasts. Harry fidgeted with his hands. His lips trembled as he slowly nodded and looked away.

"That's her," he said.

The blanket back in place, the mortuary assistant wheeled the body of Evelyn Oatley away.

Despite a lack of clear leads, the police were not idle in their hunt for the killer. For Cherrill, there was little he could do. He had compared the prints taken from the evidence found at the scene of Evelyn Hamilton's murder to those lifted from the belongings of Evelyn Oatley. Although a match eluded him, it failed to rule out the possibility that one man committed both murders. Investigators, meanwhile, scoured the victims' backgrounds, looking for even the slightest connection between the two women. Their efforts again yielded no results. One kept to herself and moved within the circles of the intelligentsia. The other struggled to make ends meet through rougher circumstance. Detective Chief Inspector Edward Greeno had been summoned from Scotland Yard's Murder Squad to coordinate the two investigations. An investigator of vast experience, Greeno had substantial contacts in the underworld. His war had thus far been a busy one, tackling a violent teenage gang in North London, going undercover to infiltrate a ring of thieves stealing ration books, and heading other investigations against numerous forms of criminality that took advantage of the city's wartime chaos. For his current task, he established his headquarters at Tottenham Court Road Police Station because it lay within the central proximity of the killer's stalking ground.

Already, he had detectives traipsing through the city's seedier neighborhoods. They questioned pimps of known violent dispositions and waded through London's human detritus in the hopes finding other viable leads. Although the murder of a prostitute was not wholly uncommon, the brutality of these specific crimes placed them on a grisly pedestal. Indeed, the files of Scotland Yard were peppered with the unsolved slayings of streetwalkers, though Evelyn Hamilton clearly was not one. Greeno realized that London was a criminal's Shangri-la. Trains chugged in and out of the city at an unrelenting pace, dropping off and carrying away multitudes of military personnel, businessmen and those simply coming to the capital to partake in the grand adventure. Troop and supply ships continually sailed in and out of the city's ports. There would be little challenge for one to sneak into the city, do whatever one planned to do and then vanish.

The nature of the victims in question also added to the challenge of Greeno's task. Although a woman of respectable means, Evelyn Hamilton lived the life of a quiet loner with no firm social anchoring. Evelyn Oatley, though a loner in the emotional sense, moved in shadowy circles. Her profession added a complexity to the case, for it brought her into contact with countless men. Tracing the customers of a working girl proved to be no small task, especially in Lon-

don where military personnel constituted the majority of a
prostitute's clientele.

American and British servicemen, once inducted, viewed
gruesome films designed to mute their lustful urgings. Cel-
luloid introduced them to the unpleasant symptoms of gon-
orrhea, syphilis and other diseases that mutated men into
drooling, blistering wreckage. But the deterring effect of
such films was temporary at best. Military men on leave
flooded Soho and congregated in Piccadilly Circus looking
to buy sex, a commodity in ample supply. Greeno often
strolled the streets in the evening and watched the illicit
business transactions taking place in many West End doorways and on most street corners. Such activity placed the
women in greater danger than the men, and the end result
might be—as the Yard's files made clear—a butchered
heap left to rot in a dirty bed in some squalid flat. The file
remained open on one working girl found in the West End
with an axe buried in her skull.

The press had yet to jump on the two recent killings. Wartime London had enough going on to adequately divert the
attention of roving newsmen elsewhere. But like scandalous
high-society gossip eagerly passed from one diamond-
wearing socialite to the next, word of the murders spread
from street corner to street corner and became *the* topic of
working-girl conversation. The details of both murders grew
increasingly horrific as word passed from ear to ear. Now
women took more notice of their surroundings. The echo of
footsteps down a deserted alley or soft footfalls along a quiet
street invoked a new kind of dread. Returning to a room or
ducking away in the shadows for a loveless encounter always carried a heavy element of risk. But the recent murders
underscored the dangers involved.

And what of the killer? What twisted malignancy within

drove him to do such things? Perhaps not even the killer himself knew. The RAF men barracked at St. James's Close—in Flat 27, Room B—were oblivious to the secret life of Gordon Frederick Cummins. Although vain and pompous, he never displayed a dark underside. And despite what some considered an annoying personality, Cummins always seemed to be in good cheer. A Player's cigarette permanently attached itself to his lips, which seemed forever curved in a smile. On nights of leave, he boasted the same debauched enthusiasm as everyone else for the drink and ladies. Over the past couple of days, he had raised some eyebrows with the amount of cash he waved around. Subsequently, men who disliked him buried their grudges long enough to take advantage of his generosity. But beneath Cummins's refined surface and obscured by the aristocratic speech, there lurked something as cold and dark as a February midnight. It writhed just below the skin and compelled him to do things. He could not remember when he first fell victim to such compulsions, yet when they took hold, their power overwhelmed him. They subjugated all thought and reason. A great pressure built in his head and groin, forcing him to act. It was a violent sexual charge, and one that the civilities and gentle lovemaking of marriage had no chance of satisfying.

His wife's name was Marjorie, and she lived in a flat on Westmoreland Road, Barnes. They had married on December 28, 1936, at the Paddington Register Office just one year after Cummins had joined the ranks of the RAF. The two had met in May 1936 at Empire Air Day in Henlow. Once married, they rented a flat and Cummins allowed his sister-in-law, Freda, to move in. This allowed Marjorie to keep the flat and pay the rent while Cummins was off on active duty. It also meant Cummins had a proper home to come to when on leave. When Britain went to war, Cummins found himself stationed with the Marine Aircraft Experimental Establishment at Felixstowe and eventually moved with them to Scotland. He spent three years in the north, from 1936 to 1939. He quickly went about establishing a social routine for himself, searching for the best nearby pubs and restaurants, and acquainting himself with the local ladies. His fellow enlistees soon noticed the haughty manner with which Cummins carried himself. His behavior earned him the nickname "The Count." Despite being recently married, he lived the life of a carefree bachelor. He spent his evenings attending dances, where he swayed on the floor in the seductive company of various women. Sexual conquests came easy to Cummins, whose charm and dashing smile generally brushed aside any reservations or moral guidelines a woman might have.

On October 25, 1939, Cummins transferred as a rigger to No. 600 Squadron, stationed at Helensburgh, Dumbartonshire. He continued his carnal escapades and bragged to the other cadets, offering the most salacious details of his bedroom adventures. He rendered his tales in the polished speech for which he had become known, but no longer was he referred to as "The Count." At Helensburgh, he moved up the social ladder—if only in nickname—when his peers dubbed him "The Duke." The name stuck and followed him to his next posting at Colerne, Wiltshire, in the south of England. He arrived in Colerne in April 1941 and quickly befriended one Flight Lieutenant Peate, the public relations officer for the RAF in that area. Very soon Cummins was telling Peate—and others—that he was the son of a peer. He referred to himself as the Honorable Gordon Cummins and tried to create the impression that he was the black sheep of his family. While others in his family found contentment in country weekends and sipping sherry at stuffy cocktail receptions, Cummins hungered for the smell of cordite and the danger of combat. His prowess for storytelling had all who knew him convinced that he spoke the truth. The fact he always seemed to have money at the ready only lent credence to his story. Those around him assumed he received an allowance from his rich relatives.

As he had done at his previous posting, Cummins made a name for himself with the local ladies. He boasted of the nights he had spent in the hotels of Bath, sweating up the sheets with countless women. Billeted off base during his time at Colerne, he went to live with a local farmer named Guy Fields and became quick friends with the farmer's wife. He used his charm and wiles to gain access to the farmer's car, which he drove regularly to the White Hart, the local pub and inn. Some days he felt particularly debonair and rode to the pub on one of the farmer's horses. The locals greeted him with much enthusiasm. Such friendliness had little to do with the kind nature of village folk and more to do with the fact that Cummins threw his money around. He treated everyone he could to drinks. Indeed, the "Honorable" Gordon Cummins often blew through his "family allowance" in just two days. Cummins's own tastes were expensive. His choice of drink, whenever liquor availed itself to him, was Canadian rye whiskey.

If anyone doubted Cummins's success with women, the doubts were soon cast aside after a fellow cadet saw him one evening in the lobby of a Bath hotel holding center court with a group of ladies—women not of the working-girl variety. Their manner of dress and speech indicated they were of the same social strata from which Cummins claimed to be descended. Among such women, fraternizing with members of His Majesty's Forces was a matter of pride. Members of the Royal Air Force, specifically, enjoyed a certain status other military men lacked, for RAF personnel were considered the aristocracy of the nation's defense. These women—with their fancy dresses, jewel-encrusted necks and husbands away at war—exercised high standards when inviting someone back to their homes to share their beds. Cummins thrived on sex and, when on leave, frequently ventured into London. He bragged that he ran in high social circles in the glittering West End. To those Cummins told his tales, it seemed his wife played a relatively minor role in his life. He confessed to a few people that visiting Marjorie was more of a chore than anything else. She did nothing for him. Exercising a cold indifference toward her, he only graced Marjorie with his presence when he felt light in the wallet.

When he wasn't drinking or screwing, Cummins performed his military duties in a manner that grabbed the attention of his superior officers, who frequently commented that his discipline and physical abilities surpassed those of the other men. But he truly excelled in the social exercises. Behind the backs of his commanders, Cummins often drove to Bath to visit a café—dubiously named the Hole in the Wall—which had been deemed off limits to all military personnel. He left for town dressed in his uniform, but pulled over along the way to change into civilian clothing, thus allowing him to get past the café's doorman and mingle where women of low moral caliber could be found. Through all these sordid encounters, Cummins's deadly urges remained in check. Or did they? During Cummins's time at Colerne, an airman assaulted a woman one evening in the nearby town of Ford. The victim had been unable to describe her assailant and the investigation went nowhere. Two more women were assaulted by an airman in Bath. Again, they could not provide a description of their attacker. Regardless of the perpetrator's true identity, Cummins's lust for blood was never fully realized—and he continued to charm the women he encountered, including Lieutenant Peate's wife. She regularly did Cummins's laundry and invited him to the house for dinner. Whether the extent of their relationship went beyond that, no one ever said.

Cummins's military duties took him to Predanneck, Cornwall, on November 10, 1941. The men at his new posting quickly tired of Cummins's sexual boasting, though they could not deny he had considerable influence over women and a refined taste in drink. In the nearby town of Falmouth, he joined a social club—the Blue Peter Club—and took a job assisting the proprietress behind the bar. He made an exemplary barman with his gift for conversation and quick wit. He developed a rather close relationship with the joint's proprietress, who let him use her private apartment above the club. The people he served—and his fawning boss—believed Cummins was someone of high breeding. But his behavior soon suggested otherwise when, one evening, the proprietress caught him serving free drinks to other RAF personnel. Disappointed, she quickly relieved Cummins of his bartending duties. Not long after the firing, the woman discovered about thirty-five pounds' worth of jewelry missing from her apartment. Although local police suspected Cummins, they weren't able to prove a thing.

Cummins had amassed a thousand hours of flying time by February 1942. With his taste for adventure, he decided he wanted to be a pilot. The previous September

he'd appeared before the RAF's selection board and
taken a pilot test. His exemplary performance earned him
a transfer to the Air Crew Receiving Centre at Regent's
Park. He was ordered to report there at 10 a.m. on Monday, February 2, 1942. He spent Saturday, February 1,
with his wife and sister-in-law in their flat on Westmoreland Road. Marjorie Cummins and her sister had moved
three times in an effort to find a place that might make a
suitable home for the three of them. The trio spent that
Saturday at the apartment and dined together in the evening. Cummins apologized to his wife for neglecting her
recently and explained that he had been studying hard for
his pilot's course. Marjorie—who loved her husband and
derived much joy from married life—was sympathetic.

Early on the morning of February 2, Cummins left his
home for the Air Crew Receiving Centre and was barracked at St. James's Close. He spent the following night
out on the town, picking up a girl at a pub near Oxford Circus. The morning after, the men in Rooms A and B of Flat
27 at St. James's Close played audience to Cummins's tale
of sexual aplomb, replete with hand gestures and simulated
moaning. He returned home to see his wife on Saturday,
February 7, and spent the afternoon with her. The next day,
he saw her again, taking the tube from Baker Street to
Hammersmith and then riding the bus the rest of the way.
As he sat eating dinner with Marjorie that evening, Cummins told her he needed money.

"I'm on the rocks," he said.

Marjorie smiled and gave him a pound from her purse.
He kissed her good-bye at 6:30 p.m., explaining he had to
report back to St. James's Close for guard duty. The reality
of his situation, however, was quite different. There were
no duties required of him on this specific night. Cummins's

plans instead called for another salacious evening in the West End.

Come daybreak, Evelyn Hamilton would be dead.

When Cummins awoke the next morning, he went about his daily duties with the ease of one accustomed to the monotonous routine of military life. His fellow officers-in-training noticed nothing strange in his demeanor, and he spoke of his previous night's exploits with the same gusto they now expected from him. While police responded to the gruesome find in the bomb shelter on Montague Place, Cummins was taking part in his morning drills. There was breakfast and morning inspection, and talk about what debauchery could be had on the town that night. And all the while, something grotesque stirred within him. When Cummins got out of bed on the morning of February 10, the body of pretty Evelyn Oatley lay carved and bleeding in her cramped little room.

Cummins and the other men stationed at St. James's Close received their inoculations that afternoon. At 6:30 p.m., they went to the nearby YMCA on Avenue Road. Several men saw Cummins reading a book by the fireplace. A cigarette hung lazily from his lips. He called his wife at 9 p.m. and told her the inoculation had left him feeling tired. She asked him when he would be home again, and he said he would try and visit the following weekend. He hung up and conversed briefly with James Granfield, an airman he'd met two years prior while stationed in Yorkshire. Granfield was putting on his coat and getting ready to return to the barracks.

"You're not going out tonight?" Cummins asked.

"It's too much near payday," Granfield said.

Cummins laughed, thrust a hand into his pocket and pulled out a thick roll of pound notes. "Would you like to borrow some money? There's twenty-five pounds here."

Granfield was curious as to where Cummins came into so much cash, but thought it rude to ask. He politely declined Cummins's offer and returned to St. James's Close, leaving Cummins to venture out on the town solo.

On the afternoon of February 11, Inspector Leonard Clare went through the travel case Evelyn Hamilton had left behind at the Three Arts Club. Its contents—papers and other documents relating to pharmacology; makeup; some clothes and a handkerchief bearing the laundry mark "E. 2474"—appeared to be of little consequence. He made a record of the dead woman's possessions and booked it all as evidence.

Detective Chief Inspector Greeno, meanwhile, settled into the recently established center of operations at the Tottenham Court Road Police Station. No stranger to murder and the workings of such multifaceted investigations, Greeno was one of the Murder Squad's most revered investigators. The squad's name was not an official designation, but rather a nickname assigned by the public. When the squad came into existence, there had been seven hundred detectives working in London at the exclusion of nearly everywhere else in the country. Rural and county police departments had not been properly trained or equipped to handle the grim task of tackling murder. Home Secretary Herbert Gladstone suggested that—should the need arise—Scotland Yard take over the investigations of violent crimes from smaller agencies. A number of detectives from the Yard's Criminal Investigation Department were to be made available through the Home Office for this very purpose. Before long, the name Murder Squad attached itself to the men, and their morbid work had captured the public's imagination.

Now in his temporary office, Greeno went to a large wall map of Central London and stuck in two colored pins to mark the scenes of the murders. He had no doubt the killer would do it again, for sexual sadists keep feeding their perverse appetites until they are captured or killed. Greeno had reviewed Cherrill's report, explaining that fingerprint evidence indicated the killer of both women was left-handed. Evelyn Hamilton had been practice, Greeno believed. But something prevented the killer from seeing that violent act through to its bloodied and mutilated conclusion. But with Evelyn Oatley, the perpetrator had the luxury of a private room and little risk of distraction. He violated her with the torch and appeased his sickening appetite with the mutilation of her body. Such needs are satisfied for only so long before the perverse urgings take hold once again. Greeno knew this and waited for the killer's next outburst.

SEVEN

Barbara Lowe was only fifteen when a maniac butchered her mother. For the first five years of her life, Barbara lived with her parents—Fred and Margaret Lowe—in a small house in Southend-on-Sea. Her father owned a fancy-goods store called the Beach Bazaar, where her mother worked as an assistant. In 1932, when Barbara was five, her father died. In the years just prior to his death, Fred Lowe's business dealings had turned sour, resulting in bankruptcy. Margaret Lowe had been forced to sell the family business and home furnishings in a futile attempt to make ends meet. To further pay off the mounting debt, Margaret took a job as a housecleaner before moving to London in 1934 in the hopes of finding better work. Her move to the metropolis proved to be a solo endeavor, as she thought it best if her daughter stay behind. It had been a decision made with Barbara's best interests in mind. And so—with her daughter enrolled in St. Gabriel's boarding school—Margaret Lowe disembarked at Victoria Station in a city she was not entirely unfamiliar with.

Even to those who thought they knew her, Margaret Lowe remained something of an enigma. Her brother-in-law, William, knew her as "Peggy." William Lowe had always looked upon his brother's wife with an air of suspicion. He sometimes doubted whether the couple had ever been joined in matrimony. Fred Lowe had been married once before, to a woman named Alice, who died in 1918. Visiting his brother two years after Alice's death, William had been surprised to find Fred living with another woman.

"He said to me, 'This is my wife; we have been married at a Register Office,'" William later told authorities. The woman had been introduced to him as "Peggy"—and for the fourteen years he maintained contact with her, William never knew his supposed sister-in-law by any other name. What little he did know about her came from Peggy herself. She told him on one occasion she had been a chorus girl at the Gaiety Theatre prior to marrying Fred. She also said she enjoyed going into London on frequent shopping trips. William doubted this, for money had often been a major concern of his brother's. Furthermore, these frequent shopping trips never seemed to result in new possessions around the house. William believed his brother's "wife" worked as a prostitute. These alleged shopping forays into the city served no other purpose than to provide an alibi. It gave her an excuse to escape the boredom of domesticity and spread her legs for a few strangers willing to pay for a romp. William, sensitive to his brother's feelings, smartly kept his theory to himself. Barbara entered the picture in 1927, much to William's surprise. The couple said they rescued the young girl from an orphanage, yet according to his statement to detectives, William never recalled his brother discussing plans to adopt a child.

William last saw Peggy two years after his brother's death in 1932 and just prior to her departure for London. Peggy and Barbara lived together in a small flat and took in boarders to try and pay the bills. When that failed, Peggy enrolled Barbara in boarding school and left for the metropolis. She wrote to William and informed him she had sold the Beach Bazaar and the family's home furnishings. When William wrote to her expressing concern for his brother's business affairs, he only received an angry response telling him to mind his own business. The next time he saw Peggy, she was lying on a metal slab and known by a different name.

The ladies who worked the streets of London's West End dubbed her "The Lady" because of her refined ways. She wore clothes and spoke in a manner far removed from one who sold sex for a living. By the time of her death, she had been working as a prostitute for at least fifteen years. She always worked alone, and began her nightly duties after 11 p.m. Charing Cross Road and Oxford Street were two of her favorite prowling grounds, and she could often be found flaunting her assets in a Charing Cross pub called the Excelsior. One woman who knew "The Lady" in passing from their time on the streets was Kathleen Norah, a one-time Lyon's waitress who moved from one type of service industry to another in 1938 to make more money. It had been at that time—while hustling in Piccadilly Circus—that Kathleen first met "The Lady," a woman who stood out from the other working girls. "The Lady" kept to herself and had a penchant for felt hats and fur coats. On most nights she appeared drunk, though she was never seen frequenting any of the Piccadilly pubs. She worked the

streets almost every night, strolling along the curbside of
the pavement, singing softly to herself.

On Tuesday, February 10, 1942, Kathleen hustled in
Piccadilly. The police were out in force and having a negative impact on business. The recent murders had cramped
Kathleen's style, for soliciting under the watchful eye of
"the bogies" was not conducive to making money. Potential clients scampered past without so much as a glance,
and Kathleen—incapacitated by her fear of arrest—did
nothing to attract their attention. She had gone the day before to the Marylebone Registration Office to have ration
books stamped for her and her daughter. Having taken care
of the food situation, she had hoped to make a few extra
quid and supplement the bland wartime rations with some
black-market treats. A pair of silk stockings would also be
nice. She hung around "the 'dilly" for about half an hour
before deciding to let things cool off. At 8 p.m., she went
into the Eros News Cinema. She emerged an hour later,
dismayed to see a rather uncomfortable number of policemen still milling about. Regardless, she braved the risk of
being busted and secured a date at 10 p.m. on the corner of
Shaftesbury Avenue. Kathleen never went with soldiers.
They all seemed to be cursed with the belief that something was owed them. In the bedroom—as far as her experiences went—their sexual excitement often morphed into
violence. The date she landed was a businessman whom
she took to her room at 31 Nutford Place. In less than an
hour, the deed had been done and she was primping her
hair on a Piccadilly sidewalk.

At about midnight, she found herself standing outside a
tobacco shop near the Eros News Cinema. She was waiting
to meet one of her regulars with whom she'd scheduled an
appointment at 12:30 a.m. As she watched the foot traffic

pass, a Scots guardsman approached her with money in hand. He made an offer, which she quickly rebuffed.

"I don't want to go with you," Kathleen said. "I don't go with soldiers."

The guardsman became irate and demanded Kathleen do her bit for the fighting men—all to no avail. "You just wait," he spat. "You'll enjoy yourself when the Russians get here."

As the guardsman flapped his poison tongue, "The Lady" happened to saunter by. She looked debonair in her black coat and dark-colored felt hat. She held a long cigarette in one hand and paused momentarily in front of the arguing duo. Pointing to Kathleen, she said, "You tell him you're thoroughly British." Without saying another word, she took a drag on her smoke and sauntered away. The guardsman and Kathleen watched her disappear in the darkness toward Piccadilly. The time was 12:15 a.m. To Kathleen, the woman presented an intriguing mystery, an impenetrable vault of stories and experience—one that Kathleen was keen to crack open. Unfortunately, that opportunity would never avail itself to her.

Margaret Lowe—known as "Peggy" to some and "The Lady" to others—strolled casually toward Piccadilly and her violent end. She lit another cigarette and inhaled a deep lungful of smoke. Word of the recent murders had put many working girls on edge, but Margaret carried herself with the same cool demeanor for which she was known. A lot of women in Margaret's trade loitered together in groups, seeking safety in numbers. Margaret, however, preferred to work alone. She was not ignorant to the dangers of her profession, for she had been roughed up before. She had emerged from those dealings battered and bruised, and—she hoped—a little smarter. But she always returned to the streets. What choice did she have? She had a daughter to provide for and boarding-school tuition to pay. The other avenues of business she had explored all proved to be dead ends. Margaret assessed the police situation as she emerged onto Shaftesbury Avenue. She resigned herself to a slow evening, not realizing someone had assessed her looks and decided she was to his liking. He approached her as she lit a fresh smoke. Athletic in build, he spoke with a sophisticated accent. He asked Margaret where they could go to take care of business. Margaret suggested her place.

It was just shy of one o'clock on the morning of Wednesday, February 11.

There was no question in Florence Bartolini's mind what her neighbor at 9/10 Gosfield Street did for a living. Florence lived in flat No. 1 and worked as a cleaner. The woman she knew only as Miss Lowe lived in flat No. 4 and entertained men at a steady pace around the clock. The goings on in there were noisy and often turned violent. In the early morning hours of January 22, for example, between two and three, Florence was dragged from sleep by the sounds of shouting coming from her neighbor's place. Punctuating the verbal argument had been the shattering of glass and the thump of something heavy being thrown. Florence sat up in bed and listened to the chaos unfolding down the hall. Sounds of breaking furniture soon followed, eventually giving way to the slam of a door.

The ensuing moment of silence had been briskly swept aside by heavy banging and a man's voice yelling, "Let me in! Let me in!" From what Florence could hear, Miss Lowe apparently surrendered to the man's demands and allowed him back into her apartment. The physical confrontation immediately resumed with another riot of thuds and crashes, and what sounded like a door being ripped from its hinges. Miss Lowe's voice now pierced its way through the thunderous din with a panicked shriek: "Police! Murder! Help!" The yelling suddenly stopped, and Florence—with blankets pulled up to her chin—heard heavy footsteps descending the stairs and running into the street. Beyond her bedroom window, she could hear the man beating a path in the direction of New Cavendish Street. The sound of lighter footsteps descending the stairs came to her less than two minutes later. Outside, on the pavement, Miss Lowe began calling for the police. When it became apparent her screams were going unnoticed, she returned to her flat.

Florence lay back down, only to be disturbed again within the hour when those heavy footsteps returned up the stairs. They stopped in front of Miss Lowe's apartment. Florence braced herself for the inevitable sounds of battle—but they never came. Instead, her neighbor's tormentor descended the stairs, exited the building and faded down the street. Florence saw Miss Lowe the following afternoon talking to another neighbor outside her apartment. The door to Miss Lowe's flat was smashed.

"Did you hear the noise last night?" Lowe asked Florence.

Florence said she had.

"A Canadian soldier broke into my flat and tried to murder me," Lowe said, inviting Florence in to take a look at the damage. Inside, lamps were broken, chairs overturned, and the lock on the front door had been ripped from the doorjamb. The connecting tube to the gas fire had been severed, allowing gas to escape into the room. The living room window had been smashed, and pieces of jagged glass littered the carpet.

"He was a dirty piece of work," said Lowe, referring to her assailant. She lifted her shirt and showed Florence the dark bruises on her chest and stomach. A large, purplish black splotch colored the skin beneath her chin. "I didn't even know the man. He was a complete stranger—a boy of perhaps nineteen or twenty."

"Did you call the police?" Florence asked.

"No," Miss Lowe replied. "What's the good of that? I expect he's gotten away by now."

Another incident occurred shortly after two in the morning of February 4, when the sounds of a nasty verbal back-and-forth woke Florence up. This time, the combatants were having it out at the top of the stairs outside Miss Lowe's apartment. The altercation seemed to be of a less violent nature than the one before. Instead of furniture being tossed about and windows breaking, the only sounds heard were of heavy boots repeatedly running up and down the stairs, accompanied by Miss Lowe's trademark scream: "Police! Murder! Help!" It seemed, judging by the continuous noise, that nobody heeded Miss Lowe's shrieks and bothered calling the authorities. The ruckus on the stairs stopped shortly after three. Immediately thereafter, a car pulled up in front of the building and then—with screaming tires—roared away. As she settled back into bed, Florence decided to keep her nose out of this one. Indeed, she saw Miss Lowe two days later taking her laundry to the cleaner. She politely kept her mouth shut. It would be the last time Florence saw her neighbor alive.

At one-fifteen on the morning of February 11, she heard Miss Lowe come home with another man. This encounter seemed to break with recent tradition, for there was no screaming or calls for the police. Florence lay in bed half-expecting to hear once again the sounds of ripping, breaking, throwing and smashing. But there was none of that—only silence. She heard the man leave Miss Lowe's apartment sometime later and walk down the stairs to the building's front door. Lying in the darkness, she listened to the man's footsteps as he casually strolled away, whistling to himself. When Florence left her flat for work at eleven that morning, she saw that the postman had left a package outside Miss Lowe's door. She thought nothing of it and went on her way.

The package would soon hint at something horrible.

EIGHT

Chief Inspector Greeno had beefed up the police presence in Soho and Paddington. Alongside uniformed constables, plainclothes detectives were working the area. They questioned girls with names like Red Rose and Fat Mary, asking them to recount anything peculiar they might have seen or heard in recent days. Detectives wanted to know if any of the girls' clients had a propensity for violence during sex, or other strange carnal fixations. For their part, the women were highly suspicious of such questions and were loath to share details with the police. While policemen questioned, policewomen acted as bait. Operating under strong backup from Scotland Yard men, undercover female officers pretending to be working girls trolled the one square mile of the killer's hunting ground, hoping to lure him into action. All this police activity was enough to make any prostitute feel uncomfortable, not unlike the thought of a rampant serial killer stalking their ranks.

Prostitution in wartime London proved to be a boom business. The recent arrival of American soldiers in the British capital meant there was more money to throw around. Some women got downright saucy with their come-ons when a Yank swaggered by and—because the Americans seemed to have more money than their British counterparts—upped their prices, too. But even the American servicemen had to abide by certain financial limitations. "Honey, I want to rent it—not buy it," Yanks quipped to girls charging exorbitant fees. Such street-corner exchanges grated on the nerves of those on London's Public Morality Council, a collection of do-gooders who sought to preserve some sense of moral righteousness during wartime. As far as the council's members were concerned, the Blitz had assisted them somewhat in their case by scaring many prostitutes off the streets. The effect, however, was temporary at best, and the easing up of the German air assault meant street corners were once again busy with illicit dealings. The somewhat convoluted laws against prostitution really did nothing to thwart the trade. While it was illegal for a woman to solicit sex from a man, it was not illegal for her to work as a prostitute. The vast majority of women working the streets did so on a freelance basis—they answered only to themselves. A few women, however, worked in the employ of a pimp. A step up from street-level workers were the women of the high-priced brothels, establishments of ill repute that were frequented by more than several members of Parliament and other gentlemen of esteemed character. One such business on Dover Street had been the target of an investigation headed by Greeno in 1938.

The detective had then been a member of Scotland Yard's Flying Squad, formed in the wake of the first world war. To tackle London's increasingly violent breed of criminal, the squad's detectives patrolled London in cars once used by the Royal Flying Corps—hence the squad's name. The use of such vehicles changed the face of crime fighting and introduced the London public to the spectacle of high-speed chases, some of which concluded in spectacular fashion, with getaway cars somersaulting in the streets or being rammed off the roads by determined lawmen. It was while with the Flying Squad that Greeno had been summoned to Lingfield racecourse by one of his underworld contacts. In whispered tones, the informant told the detective he would find a brothel on Dover Street catering to a clientele from Britain's upper social and political circles. Greeno fed this information to his superiors and was quickly summoned by the assistant police commissioner, who ordered Greeno to get on the case. His assignment: Watch the establishment and find out who was making use of its services. One had to step carefully in a matter such as this, the assistant commissioner said. One wrong move and a government sex scandal would ensue. The government, reeling from the fallout over the Munich Agreement, was already in a fragile state. Who knew what another blow to its prestige would do?

Before anything could be done, the police needed to learn more. The Yard sent an undercover detective posing as a customer into the brothel. He was to gather information on the place, but had been instructed in no uncertain terms to keep his hands—and other parts of his body—to himself. Word came back that a six-foot Jamaican woman named Carmen Rosena, who enjoyed wearing thigh-high boots and nothing else, ran the place. And, yes, members of Parliament were indeed availing themselves of the forbidden pleasures within. The time came for Greeno—a man who firmly believed that all lawbreakers should be treated the same regardless of social standing—to act. But considering the dark and more pressing situation in Europe, Greeno planned his raid to spare the government maximum embarrassment.

At 8:40 on the evening in question—when he assumed most members of Parliament were having dinner with their wives or sipping drinks at their social clubs—Greeno, posing as a taxi driver, knocked on the front door of the Dover Street brothel. A woman answered to whom Greeno apologized, saying he must have wrong the address. The woman accepted Greeno's apology and began to shut the door, but was stopped from doing so when Greeno wedged his foot between the door and the doorjamb. Police entered the premises and rounded up the girls, who offered a wide bevy of excuses. Fortunately for the government, there were no members of Parliament enjoying the establishment's services at the time. To further prevent a government scandal, the ensuing court proceeding—dubbed the "Vault of Vice Trial"—was closed to the public. In the end, hard-up government ministers were forced to seek relief elsewhere. For the Flying Squad—whose detectives were trained in high-speed driving and primarily concerned with taking down armed robbers—the case was a rarity.

Prostitution wasn't something necessarily allowed in wartime London, but it was generally accepted as a product of the times. The recent murders, however, had forced police to focus more attention on the city's sex trade, with a particular eye cast toward streetwalkers and their johns. With military personnel flooding into the city on a daily basis, the suspect pool was growing at an exponential rate. If hunting criminals had taken on a new complexity in wartime, so too had the crime of murder. A body found with a gunshot wound to the back of the skull or a stab wound to the gut was easily identified as the product of foul play. But the Luftwaffe's bombs now allowed killers to conceal their work amid the carnage of war, strangling or beating their victims then hiding the bodies in the wreckage of a shattered building. Who knew how many people were buried as purported victims of the Blitz when, in actuality, their demise had been the result of something far more personal? The number of bodies being retrieved daily at the height of the German bombing made it impossible for autopsies to be conducted on all the deceased. Generally, the body was identified then turned over to the family for burial. Some people were buried in anonymous graves. Many times, the only thing left to stick in the ground was an arm or a leg. In other instances, the bodies were burned beyond recognition. But the West End killer seemed far too brazen to hide his deeds behind the work of the Germans. What struck Greeno was the murderer's apparent nerve, having killed one woman in a public air-raid shelter and slaughtering another in a flat, where neighbors could have easily heard the victim screaming.

The massive operation now under way to stop the killer presented another challenge to Scotland Yard's already overstrained resources. Manpower had been affected by the nation's call to arms, and the rationing of petrol placed a special burden on the department's mobility. Radio silence had been deemed mandatory, meaning patrolmen and detectives could not easily call for backup. And the rationing itself had given rise to an elaborate black market that fueled the city's criminality. Canteen workers stole cigarettes and candy from their employers and put them up for sale on the market at an inflated price, pocketing 100 percent of the profits. Food was stolen from restaurant kitchens and meat factories. Counterfeiting and racketeering, and fraud of all types, prospered. Many people turned to petty crime, stealing products from the market to make ends meet. Even in the bomb shelters, as the city above crumbled in debris and flame, people were not immune to the criminal impulses of others. "Shelter gangs" roamed the underground during raids, robbing and mugging. Pickpockets lurked in public shelters and pilfered from handbags and purses. Some gangs asserted control over the shelters they stalked as if laying claim to a piece of property.

When the all clear sounded, people emerged from the shelters and traipsed apprehensively home in the hopes of finding their house still standing. For those greeted by such luck, there could often be a downside. Houses left untouched by bombs and fire were prime targets for burglars, who snatched all they could while homeowners sought cover from the raids. A category of criminal particularly despised by authorities and the public was the notorious bomb lark. In perpetrating his crime, the bomb lark did not use violence—he simply cashed in on the misfortune of others. Following a raid, he would go to the National Assistance Office, claim his home had been destroyed and then collect an assistance check. Because of the massive workload, it was hard to disprove that someone had, in fact, been bombed out—especially if one claimed his or her identity papers had also gone up in flame. The lark's greed was generally his undoing. One man, convicted in February 1941, claimed he had been bombed out of his home nearly twenty times in five months. Such crimes demanded the attention of the police, who, on top of everything else, were now dealing with the hunt for a possible serial killer.

FEBRUARY 12, 1942

NINE

When Florence Bartolini returned home from work on the evening of the eleventh, the package outside Miss Lowe's front door still sat unclaimed. She paid it little mind, but found her curiosity slightly aroused when leaving for work the following morning. The parcel, simply wrapped in brown paper, had yet to be taken in.

Even before Henry Jouannet took his wife's hand in matrimony, the sixty-seven-year-old hotel manager knew of his betrothed's sexual proclivities. He'd met Doris—thirty-five years his junior—on Oxford Street in September 1935. The sidewalks were crowded, as well-to-do shoppers jostled in and out of Selfridges, John Lewis and the street's other high-end retailers. Henry had been shopping for nothing in particular that day; he merely enjoyed the city's vibrancy and was taking an afternoon constitutional. He caught sight of Doris as she stood at a bus stop, examining herself in a handheld mirror. Henry was taken by her looks, which were not unlike those of a stern headmistress, for Doris appeared somewhat older than her years. He had seen her before in the West End, in the company of different men. Now she stood alone, and he took it as an opportunity to introduce himself. The meeting was not one of innocent circumstance. Henry knew Doris to be a prostitute, though he sought to soften her reputation by later telling investigators "she was not a street-walker." It just so happened that "she had a few male friends who visited her for the purpose of intercourse." And so, on that September afternoon, Doris took Henry to her flat at 240 Edgware Road for sex. Following this paid-for encounter, the two became friends, a whirlwind courtship ensued, and the two were married at the Paddington Register Office on Harrow Road two months later.

Henry had been born in France, but came to Britain in 1904 and became a naturalized citizen. When he married Doris in November 1935, he was not in the hotel business. He had, in fact, retired and was receiving an annuity of ten pounds a month from the sale of the Grand Hotel in Concarneau, Brittany, which he had owned for five years. He had sold the property for more than two thousand pounds and was quite happy living on the monthly allowance provided by the sale. He thought Doris could live happily on it, too, and asked her to end her prostituting ways. She said she would and moved into Henry's home at 14 Bathurst Street, near Sussex Gardens. They lived there for nearly three years, during which time Henry had no reason to believe Doris was selling herself on the streets. It did not take long, however, for Doris to grow bored with the role of devoted housewife—and it was boredom that Henry feared would push Doris back into bed with strange men.

At about this time, Henry's mother died and left him an inheritance of thirteen hundred pounds. He used the money to buy a café and gave Doris a job as co-manager. The restaurant business, however, was not to their liking. They sold the café after a mere four months and sued the previous owner for lying about the bustling clientele. The couple was awarded six hundred and forty pounds and moved into an apartment in Eastbourne. Henry did his best for the eighteen months they lived there to keep Doris occupied and deafen her ears to the nightlife's siren call. They were living there when Britain went to war in September 1939 and when Paris fell to the Nazis in June the following year. With the conquest of France, Henry suddenly found himself in a precarious financial situation. His monthly annuity from the hotel sale stopped coming. The couple moved in with Doris's mother in Harrogate in September 1940 to soothe their financial pains, and Henry took a job as a staff manager at Oddendino's on Regent Street. He moved to London for the job and left Doris with her mother. He sent her an allowance of three pounds a week, but within a month, Doris was also living in the city.

And that's when the trouble began.

She took an apartment in Sussex Gardens, right across the street from where Henry rented a room. His wife's presence in the capital annoyed Henry. He knew she would find the temptations of London too strong to resist. He asked her to return to Harrogate, where Hitler's bombs posed less of a danger. She flatly refused. This was bad enough, but making it worse was the fact that she took up a separate residence. When Henry questioned Doris's reasoning for doing this, her answers proved evasive and the marriage quickly began to crumble.

"I visited her at this room on several occasions," Henry

later told police. "By the general atmosphere of the house, I came to the conclusion that my wife was drifting back to her old life."

Henry decided the only way to put things right was to leave his restaurant job and move just outside of the city. This he did, and he brought his wife with him—but the stress of it all broke his health, rendering him sexually impotent. Unable to satisfy his wife's needs, Henry knew she would soon use that excuse to propel herself back onto a street corner somewhere.

"My wife made frequent trips into London," he told investigators. "I do not know where she went, but she told me she was visiting friends. She never appeared to have very much money. I allowed her everything she wanted and I begged of her not to return to her old life."

Henry's begging proved not to be enough.

They moved a few more times, eventually taking up residence in October 1941 at the Queens Hotel in Farnborough, Hants, where Henry had been offered a job as manager and Doris was presented a chance to be his co-manager. The two were provided a suite of rooms and a combined income of nearly seven hundred pounds. Henry hoped the job would be a new beginning for the two of them, but Doris had other plans.

"My wife never seemed to settle down and give her mind to the business," Henry said. "She always wanted to be in London. She only made one visit to London from Farnborough, and that was during daylight hours. She, however, fell out with some of the customers at the Queens Hotel, with the result that I tendered my resignation and they accepted."

Henry next took a job as manager of the Royal Court Hotel in Sloane Square. Doris's reputation unfortunately followed them to the establishment like a dogged mongrel, and the hotel's owners expressly forbade her from having anything to do with the running of the Royal Court. The arrangement suited Doris just fine, for she had no desire to cater to the whims of pompous hotel guests who sniffed their wine before drinking it. Henry pleaded with her to return to her mother's place in Harrogate, but Doris made it clear she would leave London under no circumstances. Consequently, the couple took a flat at 187 Sussex Gardens on January 26, 1942. The flat had no communication link to the apartments above or below it, and the only way in was through the street entrance. On February 1, Henry assumed his duties as the Royal Court's manager. While the new job kept him busy, it did little to calm his frantic ruminations. The belief that his wife would soon return to the streets stirred Henry's panicked thoughts. The fact that his job required him to sleep at the hotel—thus providing Doris ample opportunity to go trolling for sex if she so desired—only fueled his paranoia.

Each evening he took lunch from 7 p.m. to 9:30 p.m., and returned to the flat to see Doris, who always had a bowl of hot vegetable soup waiting for him when he walked through the door. He would leave the flat after dinner and walk to Paddington Station to catch a train back to Sloane Square. From February 1 to the fateful night of February 12, Henry spent only one night—Saturday, February 7—at home with Doris. On the evening of Thursday, February 12, following his usual soup dinner, Henry grabbed his coat and kissed his wife good-bye.

"My wife said she would like a breath of fresh air and she accompanied me to Paddington Underground Station," Henry later told investigators. "My wife left me in a happy frame of mind, and I impressed upon her to return straight home, which she promised to do. Before leaving me, she asked me not to be late coming home on Friday, February 13. I arrived at my hotel at about 10 p.m. and spoke to the two cashiers for about ten minutes or quarter of an hour. The night porter took me up to my room on the fourth floor by lift, and I retired for the night."

Henry drifted off to sleep that night, not entirely ignorant of his wife's activities.

Doris waved her husband off at the train station then returned to the flat and readied herself for the evening. The weather was frigid, and the streets were slick with rain. A light snow had begun to fall near sunset. In her bedroom, Doris inspected herself in front of the mirror, not sure whether her wardrobe would entice men on this bitter evening. She pinned her hair up under a black hat. A dark-colored skirt hung down just below her knees and was complemented by a similar-colored shirt and black coat. What would Henry do if he discovered she had returned to selling herself again? He would verbally chastise her and remain in the marriage. Poor Henry. Doris loved her husband and she did truly care for him, but she found married life mundane. The monotony of their evening routine—the soup dinners, the banal conversation—grated on the nerves and numbed the mind. She shook her head and glanced in the mirror one last time. Satisfied that she looked as good as the weather would permit, she walked out of the bedroom and left her flat for the last time.

Also working the streets that night was twenty-eight-year-old Patricia Borg. Like Doris, Patricia was married, but still offered her body to those willing to slip a few pounds in her purse. She usually trolled along Edgware Road, between Titchbourne Street and Susssex Gardens.

Presently, she stood outside an empty storefront near Titchbourne Street and cast a weary eye up and down the lonely thoroughfare. She lit a cigarette for warmth, stepping out of the frigid drizzle and into the storefront's doorway. She held the burning end of her smoke to the face of her watch. It was 10 p.m. and business was lackluster. The men who did pass by in the street did so in a hurry under open umbrellas and soggy newspapers. In a way, that suited her just fine. Whatever propensity Patricia had felt that evening to secure business had been quickly dampened by the drizzle and snow. She had been lending serious thought to the idea of returning to her flat at 36 Titchbourne Street, when the airman approached.

His shoulders were hunched against the cold. A cigarette sat perched in one corner of his mouth; its smoke and the white vapor of his breath hung about his face in a wispy veil. His hair was thick and bushy, but losing its vibrancy in the wet weather. When he spoke, it was in a quiet, almost meek, voice, but one that sounded well educated. He squeezed into the doorway, beside Patricia, and held his cigarette to her face, just barely lighting her features. He skipped the formalities of greeting and small talk in favor of the proposition.

"Will you take me home with you?" he said. "I have two pounds."

Her self-acknowledged lack of initiative on this particular evening aside, Patricia had no desire to go with the airman. His mannerisms struck her as being creepy, though she couldn't exactly say why. Perhaps it was his quiet demeanor or his overeagerness to part with his money. Sales this easy always roused suspicion. Generally, there were the pleasantries of cordial—if not somewhat forced—introductions, followed by the customary haggling over the price. Military men always wanted a discount. Patricia never offered one. She looked the airman up and down and told him to go away. The airman accepted the rejection with good grace, simply nodding and asking her if she knew of anyone he might be able to go home with for the two-pound price.

"No," Patricia said, glancing away from him to indicate the conversation was nearing its end. "I don't know anyone."

The airman took a long drag on his cigarette, exhaled the smoke through his nose and stepped out of the doorway onto the rain-soaked pavement. He cast a glance up and down the street then wandered off. Patricia stayed put, unsure whether to call it a night or tough it out in the hopes that a more desirable business prospect might come along. Several minutes passed, and she could feel a decision fast approaching. She sniffed against the cold and rubbed her gloved hands together just as Doris Jouannet came along and stepped into the doorway's meager shelter. Although Patricia didn't know Doris's name, she recognized her immediately. The two had once trolled the same ground in Sussex Gardens and, occasionally, Edgware Road. The last time Patricia had seen her was about two months ago. Working the streets, one grew accustomed to seeing the same women on a regular basis. Doris, however, was more of a rarity on street corners. Patricia saw her only occasionally, with several months lapsing between each sighting.

"Hello, stranger," Patricia said.

Doris smiled and returned the salutation. There followed some brief talk about the weather and the sorry state of that evening's business. The two women gradually delved deeper into conversation, as Doris explained that she did not work the streets on a full-time basis.

"I'm living with an elderly gentleman who keeps me

and pays the rent," Doris said, "but the money he gives me isn't enough so I have to come out here and earn a few extra shillings. Of course, he doesn't know that I come out to pick up men—and when I do, I generally can't go out until late in the evening."

Another woman—whom Patricia knew as Yvonne—came along and joined the discussion. Patricia's thoughts of calling it quits for the evening were quickly waylaid, and the three women stood in the now-crowded doorway lost in animated chatter. Unlike Yvonne—whose colorful choice of vocabulary would not be uncommon in the most rough-and-tumble of seaside ports—Doris spoke with a refined tone. She gave the impression of being educated and did not really come across as a prostitute. Her clothes were too elegant for the nature of the work and, one could argue, a tad too conservative. She often wore her hair in a tight bun, which gave her the appearance of a strict disciplinarian, but she exuded warmth and humor in conversation. And so the women continued to discuss the nature of things until one of Patricia's regular clients approached and asked if she was working. Patricia answered in the affirmative and bid the other two women farewell as she took the man's arm and strolled off toward her flat. Soon thereafter, Yvonne and Doris also parted ways.

Patricia and Yvonne would survive the night. Doris would become a homicide statistic in the files of Scotland Yard.

TEN

Mary Heywood had met the British Army officer three months prior at the Universelle Brasserie in Piccadilly Circus. She had found him charming enough and had seen him on several occasions since then, meeting him at restaurants and pubs in the West End for nights on the town. His schedule was erratic because of his training, and Mary was never quite sure when the opportunity to see him would arise. When such evenings did present themselves, they were something to look forward to. Mary, aged thirty, was married, but separated from her husband, and looking for something beyond a casual acquaintance. It seemed to her the war had reduced most men to leering creatures intent on just one thing, for she had lost count of how many times the beasts had propositioned her for sex. Simply put, she was "not that kind of girl." On the afternoon of February 12, Mary received a phone call at her home at 1 Glenwood Grove, Kingsbury. At the other end of the line she heard her army-officer friend asking if she would be available to meet that evening. Of course she would. They agreed to meet at the Universelle Brasserie between eight and nine.

She arrived at the restaurant just before eight and took a seat near the bar, with a view of the entrance. Men in uniform crowded the place. Those who entered alone would soon thereafter leave with a woman firmly attached to their hip and their hands roaming freely. The Americans were proving to be most adept with the English ladies, much to the chagrin of many British soldiers. Along with their swagger and tales of Hollywood and sunsets on the beach, the Americans came with gifts—nylon stockings, chocolate and canned fruit—their British counterparts were hardpressed to match. To the annoyance of pub and restaurant owners, the Americans also came with gum—much of which wound up stuck under tables, chairs and bars after a thorough chewing. Mary, who cared little for gum, sat at her table and waited for her date, not realizing someone was keeping a close eye on her.

He sat at the bar, nursing a whiskey. The night had thus far proved to be a busy one, but that indescribable something still coursed through his veins like magma. The glass of whiskey in his hand had little to do with thirst and was more of a distraction, a way to occupy his time until he found what he desired. Whereas sometimes he had a preconceived notion of what would calm the torrent in his veins in terms of hair color and figure, there were other occasions—such as tonight—when the thing inside him offered little in the way of suggestions. Twirling the ice in his glass, he cast his glance across the bar and saw her sitting alone at a table. She was pretty in a conservative sort of way. Her dark hair fell about her shoulders, and her face was made up lightly. He immediately knew this woman to be the one, but couldn't say why. Perhaps it was instinct, or the result of some complex natural process like breathing or blinking one's eyes. He watched her for ten minutes to ensure she was alone before he made his move. Leaving his bar stool, he ran his hands down the front of his dress tunic to soften the creases as he approached the table.

"Are you waiting for somebody?"

Mary turned around in her chair and saw a young airman standing behind her. He looked slender in his dress blues and spoke with a refined accent. His hair was blond and scruffy, yet his smile was broad and creased the corners of his eyes.

"I'm sorry?" she said.

"I asked if you were waiting for someone," the airman replied.

"Yes, I have an appointment."

This hardly seemed to deter the airman, for he asked Mary if she would care for a drink while she waited. She was impressed by his confidence but all too aware of what he had in mind. Nevertheless, she surrendered to his charms.

"Yes, please," she said.

He made his way back to the bar and quickly returned with two whiskeys. He sat in the chair opposite Mary and put a glass in front of her while raising his in a jocular salute. She sipped her drink and watched the airman drain his glass in one thirsty gulp. He rolled the tumbler between his palms and held Mary's eyes with his. She found his gaze somewhat disconcerting and directed her attention to the restaurant's bustling clientele. The airman laughed.

"Why don't we go to the Trocadero and have some food," he said, making it more of a suggestion than a question.

"I told you, I have an appointment," Mary said. She took another sip of her drink.

"Oh, I'm sure we have plenty of time," the airman said, smiling. "In any case, I have to be back at my unit by ten-thirty."

Mary shifted in her chair and struggled with indecision. He was brutally handsome, but seemed overconfident—probably the result of vast sexual conquests, Mary thought. She silently reaffirmed that she would not fall prey to his wily charisma and verbally agreed to the invitation.

"Splendid," he said. "Let me get my coat."

He went to the cloakroom and retrieved his greatcoat, cap and respirator. When he returned to the table, he had the coat on and slung the respirator over his left arm. He pulled Mary's chair out for her and escorted her across Piccadilly to the Trocadero. They took a table for two in the cocktail lounge and drank a whiskey each. As she raised the glass to her lips, Mary noticed that the airman remained clad in his coat and cap. It seemed he had no intention of sticking around long. He also made no mention of food.

"Where do you live?" he asked.

"Wembley," Mary said, already regretting the acceptance of this man's invitation.

"That's a long way out," he said. "Don't you know anywhere around here where we can go?"

"No."

There followed a brief moment of uncomfortable silence. Mary put her drink down, and the airman smiled.

"Are you a naughty girl?" he asked.

"No, I am not," Mary shot back. "There's nothing like that about me!"

The airman, seemingly oblivious to Mary's hurt tone, reached into one of his coat pockets and pulled out a thick roll of cash.

"I'm not broke, you know," he said. "Let me show you something."

He began counting the bills in front of her, laying them out on the table like a dealer would a deck of cards.

"You're certainly not broke," Mary said, somewhat shocked.

"There's about thirty pounds here," he said as he continued counting. "So, you see, I have plenty of money."

The way he said it was somewhat disarming, but Mary still thought it would be best to leave. She stood up, thanked the airman for the drinks and began heading for the door, explaining to her temporary companion that she had to return to the Universelle lest she risk missing her date.

"Look," he said, pocketing the cash. "I'm training to be an officer in the RAF. If you'd be kind enough to perhaps go out with me later, I can promise you I'll show you a good time."

The man was both a cad and a charmer, seemingly able to turn one side of his personality on and the other off with all the ease of flicking a light switch. And, of course, there was that smile, which she was sure had lent itself to the seduction of countless women. It took less than a minute of silent debate before she acquiesced to his more charming side. She pulled a piece of paper and a pencil from her purse and jotted down her phone number: COL 6622.

"I might go out with you," she said, "but I will not make love to you. I don't do that for a living."

"All right," he said. "If you don't want to, I can't make you—but you are a nice girl and I do fancy you. I have been watching you, and I like everything about you. I really do want you."

Well, he certainly had moxie.

"I'm sorry, it's no use," Mary said. "I don't do that sort of thing."

The airman shrugged. He picked up his respirator, which had been resting against one of the table legs, and began walking with Mary toward the door. The time, according to a clock on the wall, was 9:05 p.m. They exited onto the darkened street and walked side by side. Beyond the blacked-out windows and blank facades of the buildings, people could be heard enjoying the evening. Such noise always struck a strange chord, for the voices—disembodied in the darkness—were imbued with a haunting quality and seemed to belong more to an era before the war. After walking a block, the airman suddenly stopped and turned to Mary.

"Do you know that I knocked a girl out once?" he said.

"Why would you do that?"

"Because her old man interfered, you see," the airman said. "I kicked him in the privates and then knocked her out."

There seemed to be no point to this strange admission, and the airman seemed content not to offer one. Instead, he turned in the direction they had been heading and started walking again.

"We better get you back to the brasserie," the airman said. "We'll go in the Jermyn Street entrance."

Mary—growing ever more fascinated by this stranger whose name she still did not know—followed. She found it increasingly difficult to find her way. Never sure of her footing in the dark, she reached into her purse and pulled out a small electric torch. She turned it on and shone the weak light on the ground in front of her.

The airman stopped again.

"You don't want to use that," he said, taking the torch from Mary and switching it off. He gave it back to her and told her to return it to her purse.

By way of Windmill Street, they crossed Piccadilly along

the west side of Haymarket, then turned right and began walking down the south side of Jermyn Street away from the Universelle.

"You're taking me the wrong way round," Mary said.

"I want to kiss you good night," the airman said. "Aren't there any air raid shelters around here?"

"I don't know of any," Mary said. "In any case, I wouldn't go in one with you."

Why she was still walking with the man, she couldn't really say. But, against her better judgment, she followed him as he turned left onto St. Alban's Street. They did not walk long before they came to the Captain's Club, where the airman pulled Mary into a doorway just off the street. The gesture was not threatening in nature, but rather playful. The airman put his respirator down by his feet and put his arms around Mary's waist. He kissed her without meeting any resistance, but that changed when his hands slid quickly from her hips to just beneath her skirt.

"You must not do that," Mary said, trying to push his hands away.

The airman said nothing and his hands stayed in place, moving only when Mary struck hard at his wrists. Angry, she turned toward the street, but was yanked back into the doorway. The airman positioned himself so as to block her escape and took her face in his hands. Mary opened her mouth to protest, only to find his squeezing fingers suddenly wrapped around her throat. She grasped frantically at the man's clothing and face, searching for something to claw or hit. The greater she struggled, the tighter his grip became. She tried to scream but could only emit a hoarse gasping sound as the man's fingers dug deeper into the flesh of her neck. Her throat began to close and her arms grew heavy. Her hands lacked the strength to maintain their desperate action. A thick gurgling noise was now the only sound escaping her mouth—but she could hear another sound, too.

It came from the airman.

He was talking, but his voice was distant and trance-like. "You won't, you won't," he said. "You won't, you won't . . ."

The grip on Mary's throat tightened as her attacker continued mumbling. Her arms were near deadweights and moved with insufficient force and speed when she attempted to claw his eyes. Consciousness slowly began slipping away as blackness moved in from the periphery of her vision. Her lungs heaved and her tongue thrashed between her teeth. The airman's face was the last thing she saw before everything succumbed to the advancing darkness. His features were eerily calm and lacked any hint of emotion. All the while, he continued his bizarre muttering: "You won't, you won't, you won't, you won't . . ."

John Shine, an eighteen-year-old night porter, walked through St. James's Market in the direction of Regent Street. The novelty of the blackout had long since worn away for the young man, and he longed for the return of the city's nighttime dazzle. The street was relatively quiet with only a few passersby, so it was sheer luck he happened to wander by the doorway near the Captain's Club at that specific moment. The time was 9:45 p.m.

The flicker of an electric-torch light just off the street and in a doorway down a shallow side alley caught Shine's attention. Intrigued, he crossed the street, moved in that direction, and as he did, he heard what sounded like a scuffle. The light went on again—then, just as quickly, it was gone.

The light flashed on a third time as he got closer, and illuminated the legs of a woman lying across the doorway. Suddenly, someone ran out of the darkness, dropping the torch before disappearing around the corner of St. Alban's Street. Shine ran toward the lady. He fumbled in a pocket for his matches and lit one. The lady lay with her head against the door and her feet pointing toward the roadway. Her skirt was pulled up, revealing the tops of her stockings and the clips of her suspenders. Her dress had been torn open and a couple of the buttons appeared to be missing. She was groaning, saying something incoherent. Her face was dirty and smeared with blood. Shine knelt beside her.

"What's wrong?" he asked. "Are you okay?"

The woman just continued to moan.

Shine ran into the street and yelled for help. A lady stepped forward and inquired as to what was the matter. Shine led her to the injured woman. The lady volunteer looked at Mary lying on the ground and became indignant. Women who threw themselves at any man in uniform were just asking for trouble. The whole world had gone insane, and with that collapse in sanity so, too, had come a decay of morals. Women were openly flaunting their wares on the street and getting drunk in pubs. It was disgusting, and she let her distaste for it be known.

"I have seen this woman in a pub," she said. "She has been drinking with an airman."

She walked away and left a shocked John Shine to handle the situation by himself.

Not bothering to find further assistance, Shine bent down and helped the battered lady to her feet. Her legs were weak, and she nearly tumbled to the ground when she tried to walk. Shine leaned her gently against the wall.

"Are you all right?" he asked.

She raised a hand to her face and dabbed at the blood on her lips with trembling fingers.

"Oh, my bag," she said. It was lying on the ground with its contents scattered about her feet. She began to cry. "What has he done?"

Shine bent down to pick up the bag and noticed a respirator lying in the doorway. He picked it up and asked the lady if it belonged to her. She said no. With the respirator slung over his shoulder—and forgetting about the woman's bag and other possessions—Shine suggested he take her to the hospital. The woman agreed, and the two of them began walking slowly toward Haymarket. Although the woman's legs had regained some sense of solidity, they remained far from steady. Shine allowed the woman to lean against him to prevent her from falling.

Police Constable James Skinner was at the intersection of Haymarket and Piccadilly at 9:50 p.m. when he saw a battered woman leaning against a young man who seemed to be doing his utmost to keep the lady upright. Skinner approached the couple, curious as to the circumstances surrounding the woman's condition.

"This lady was attacked by a man in uniform," Shine said. "I didn't see who did it, but I have his gas mask."

"Where did this happen?" Skinner asked.

Shine pointed over his shoulder and said, "Around the back of St. James's Market."

Skinner turned his attention to the woman. "Would you like me to accompany you to the hospital or West End Central Police Station?"

"The police station," the woman said in a shaky voice.

Together with Shine, Skinner walked the woman to the police station on Saville Row, where they met with Detective Sergeant Thomas Shepherd. Mary gave Shepherd her name and recounted for him all that had transpired. Shine handed over the respirator, while Skinner went to the scene of the attack and found Mary's bag lying outside No. 1 St. James's Market. Having taken Mary's statement, Shepherd had an officer escort her to the hospital. He questioned Shine, thanked him for his time and examined the respirator. It was a service respirator carried in a haversack with an RAF Regimental number—525987—printed on the inside of the flap. Shepherd reached for a phone and dialed the RAF Police at Abbey Lodge, Regent's Park, not realizing the significance of the evening's events.

Charles Johnson was a corporal in the RAF. Like Gordon Frederick Cummins, he was attached to A Squadron and billeted at St. James's Close in Regent's Park. Johnson knew Cummins only in passing. The two never socialized and Johnson knew nothing of the other man's habits, though he had heard plenty of talk regarding Cummins's aristocratic demeanor and way with the ladies. On this particular night, Johnson was serving as orderly sergeant at the billet. He commenced duty at 6 p.m. and would remain on duty until six the following morning. Among Johnson's responsibilities was ensuring that those who were meant to be in their billets at a certain time were indeed there, and preventing those who did not have leave time from sneaking out. The evening had so far been quiet.

The phone in the orderly sergeant's room jangled on its hook at 10:30 p.m. Johnson picked it up and was somewhat surprised to hear an officer from the RAF Service Police on the other end of the line.

"I need you to search records and trace the number of

an airman," the investigator said. "The number is 525987. Do you have that?"

Johnson grabbed a pencil and scribbled the number down on a sheet of paper. "Yes, I have it."

It did not take Johnson long to sort through the personnel files and find the requested information. "I ascertained that the number given to me was allotted to LAC Cummins of 14/32 Flight," Johnson told investigators. "I sent an orderly room runner to Cummins's room to see if he was there, but I was informed he was out."

Johnson relayed the information to the RAF Service Police, who in turn contacted Detective Sergeant Thomas Shepherd at West End Central Police Station. Shepherd then placed a call through to Johnson at 11:30 p.m. and asked him to make sure Cummins was detained when he returned to his billet, as he was wanted for questioning in a police matter. Without going into specifics, Shepherd told Johnson that Cummins was being sought in connection with an assault of a woman in the West End. Johnson assured the detective that the police would be notified as soon as Cummins returned and hung up the phone.

For the time being, Shepherd had done all he could.

ELEVEN

Catherine Mulcahy loitered in the darkness of Piccadilly Circus waiting for someone to come along. She had called London home for the past ten years, having moved to the capital with her family when she was fifteen. She was married, but liked to assert the fact that she had money of her own. She lived at 29 Southwick Street and would often "take a man into my flat for the purposes of sexual intercourse." On those occasions when she wasn't too sure of the man she was with, she would take him to a secondary location at a room near Marble Arch. This prevented any undesirables from learning where she lived. It was not uncommon at times for some of her crazier customers to show up at her front door unannounced to demand amorous attention during her off hours.

By the evening of Thursday, February 12, Catherine knew of the West End killings. Gossip on the street suggested that the killer's inspiration was the grisly work of a more notorious slayer who once stalked the slums of London's East End. How much of this was rumor and how much was fact Catherine didn't know—but it hardly mattered. The barbaric reign of Jack the Ripper in 1888 had fueled a media frenzy complete with graphic accounts of the crimes and bizarre rumors as to the killer's identity. In 1940s London, the work of this latest slasher was being sidelined by larger events on a global scale. In pubs across the country on this particular evening, the main topic of conversation was not the razor-slashing antics of a madman, but a humiliating defeat in home waters for the Royal Navy. Earlier in the day, the dreaded German battleships *Scharnhorst* and *Gneisenau* had slipped from the French port of Brest—where they were undergoing repair work—braved the coastal gun batteries of Dover, evaded the RAF and Royal Navy and managed to return to Germany.

Had the whole world not descended into madness, the killer's activities would surely have garnered sensational headlines. Unlike his Victorian predecessor, the West End killer worked at a frantic pace, slaying in the course of a week nearly the same number of women Jack the Ripper eviscerated in three months. But where as the West End killer worked in anonymity, Jack the Ripper sought attention for his crimes with letters to the media. The Victorian killer's lust for publicity and written theatrics only served to fuel the media's insatiable appetite for the story. On the evening of February 12, 1942, John Shine's curiosity and his unintended rescuing of Mary Heywood had only fueled the West End slayer's need to kill.

Catherine stood outside Oddendino's in Piccadilly when the airman approached her shortly before 10 p.m. In the blackout, his facial features were just barely distinguishable in the weak orange glow of the cigarette hanging loosely from his lips. He stood silently in front of Catherine and took a long drag on his smoke, expelling a thick cloud with a lengthy hiss. He took another step closer and—as he was prone to do—held the glowing end of his cigarette up to the woman's face. He liked what he saw. Her hair was a dark blond. Her face was full, but not heavy, and she had the build of a nicely curved woman.

"Will you go with me?" he said.

"Yes," Catherine replied. "It will cost you two pounds."

"Where do you live?" the airman asked as he handed the money to her.

Her experiences on the streets had endowed Catherine with a sixth sense. Some men gave off a certain vibe that opened a nervous pit in her core. It might be the way they avoided eye contact, or simply the way they carried themselves. Men who walked with quick, shuffling steps were often nervous and had something to hide. Men with hands thrust deep in their pockets, shoulders hunched and their gaze locked firmly on the ground were burdened by guilt. These were not theories deduced from a textbook, but lessons learned on darkened street corners and under well-worn sheets. One had to be careful in this line of work, remaining tuned in to the character of others so as to get an immediate sense of what lurked beneath the surface. Almost at once, the airman gave her a bad vibe—though she wasn't exactly sure why. Perhaps it was his straightforward approach. There was also something about the way he looked, though perhaps not in the physical sense. He was smiling, but his eyes conveyed no emotion. In the faded glow of his cigarette, it was like looking through a window into a dark hollow space. He also seemed harried and slightly out of breath. On a more basic level, the acquisition of his business had been too easy. He had agreed too quickly on the price. The combination of all these things made Catherine feel as if countless hairy-legged spiders were skittering across her skin. Nevertheless, she needed the money and was willing to take a risk—but she wouldn't do it in her home. When he asked her where she lived, Catherine was quick to offer a lie.

"I live near Piccadilly," she said, "but a friend of mine is there right now using the phone."

The airman nodded.

"I can take you to my room near Marble Arch," she said.

The airman again nodded and eyed her through a freshly exhaled cloud of smoke. "I'll get us a taxi," he said. One place was just as good as any other for what he had in mind. A surface air-raid shelter would have sufficed. A few minutes were all he needed to satisfy his frenzied cravings. The evening's previous efforts had done little to appease the gnawing hunger in his gut. The hair on his body bristled and his skin perspired beneath the rough cotton of his uniform. His groin felt hot and the percussion of his heart reverberated against his ribs. A heavy pulse beat out an arrhythmic cadence between his temples and made his head ache. He hailed a cab, and the two of them climbed into the backseat. When the taxi driver asked for an address, Catherine gave him the Marble Arch location. She made an attempt to engage the airman in small talk as the taxi pulled away from the curb. She liked to establish some sort of connection with her clients, if only to present herself as a human being and to disarm any strange urges they might have.

"I'd really like to make five pounds tonight," she said.

"Don't worry," the airman said. "I have thirty pounds."

He pulled the thick wad of paper money from his pocket. He retrieved two one-pound notes from the roll and handed them to Catherine. She promptly stuffed them in her purse. The casualness with which the airman parted with his money also put Catherine on edge, though it did nothing to quell her willingness to accept it. No sooner had she pursed the money, than the airman was kneeling on the taxi's floor in front of her. Mindless of the driver, he lifted Catherine's skirt and buried his face between her thighs. He was ravenous and his movements were rough.

"You mustn't," Catherine said, trying to push the airman's head away. "Not here."

The driver kept his eyes on the road, his mouth shut, and fought the urge to stare too long in the rearview mirror. All the while, Catherine pulled at the airman's scruffy blond hair in a futile attempt to get him back in his seat. It wasn't anything the driver hadn't seen before. These military types could get pretty raunchy when they wanted to, and it never ceased to amaze him how all decorum went south when their urges kicked in. The airman, however, did stop, and returned to his seat without so much as saying a word. Catherine shot the young man an angry glance as she straightened her clothing. They sat in silence until the taxi passed Hyde Park.

"Why don't we get out here and have some fun in the park?" the airman said.

"Don't be silly. We'll be at my room soon."

Hyde Park was a notorious gathering ground for prostitutes, who would guide men to them by whistling in the darkness. Catherine, however, preferred working the city streets. In the dark, Hyde Park was a desolate expanse of meandering walkways, thick shrubbery and long air-raid trenches—all of which were ideal locations for bad and violent things to be done without having to worry about interference from other people.

The taxi passed Marble Arch and turned down a narrow side street, eventually stopping in front of a drab, squat building. The airman got out, paid the driver and extended a helping hand to Catherine. They stood on the sidewalk and watched the taxi disappear round a corner. Catherine was having second thoughts, but she knew to deny the airman her services now—after enthusiastically pocketing his money—would in all likelihood incur his wrath. She led him into the building without further hesitation and up to her room. When they got there, she lit the gas fire and turned the knob on the meter to her electric light. The light momentarily bathed the room in a pathetic yellow glow before suddenly going out.

"Do you have a shilling for the meter?" she asked.

The airman, standing in the center of the room, answered in the negative without ever checking his pockets.

Catherine walked into the kitchen and put the money the airman had given her in an old tin. She took a saucepan from a cupboard and returned to the bedroom with it. There, she took piece of paper, placed it in the saucepan and lit it with a match. The paper flared briefly then extinguished itself, once again leaving the room in near darkness except for the glow of the electric fire.

"Why did you do that?" the airman asked, as he began taking off his clothes.

"I just wanted a bit more light," she said.

The airman, now naked, stood watching her as she took off her clothes, leaving on only her boots and a necklace made of nine large beads shaped like flowers. He liked the look of the jewelry against her skin and the stark contrast of black boots against white flesh. She was exposed. His breath came and went in a quickening rasp. Sweat dripped down his inner thighs and the crease in the center of his back. His hands grew clammy. He followed her with his eyes as she moved to the bed, picked up his clothing and placed it on a nearby chair. She pulled down the sheets and lay across the mattress. Her blond hair splayed out around her, she beckoned him closer with a curled index finger.

"I want you to lie on the floor," the airman said. He had particular tastes.

Catherine refused. She just wanted to make her five pounds for the night and do it without having to bend her body like some carnival contortionist. She told him the bed would be fine, and the airman moved slowly toward her without making further demands. He kneeled at the foot of the bed and began kissing the warm flesh of Catherine's inner legs, slowly moving his fingers upward to explore the soft pasture of her sex. Catherine lay still and kept silent, eager to be done with it and have this man out of her room. He said nothing as his hands traversed skin that crawled beneath his touch. The feel of his lips turned her cold inside.

"Would you like to get on top?" she said, hoping to move the process along.

The airman crawled up onto the bed and loomed over Catherine on his hands and knees. She reached under the pillow and pulled out a preventative. She rolled the condom on, signaling it was time for him to get down to business. The airman, however, didn't move. He instead began to idly fondle her breasts without comment. In the darkness, Catherine tried to get some read on the airman's thoughts, which became suddenly clear when he brought his weight down on her body. He slammed both knees into her stomach and knocked the wind from her lungs. At the same time, he brought his hands to her throat and pressed his thumbs into her windpipe. He moved with remarkable speed and said nothing as he began choking the life out of her.

Catherine managed to scream once before the fingers at her throat silenced her voice. She clawed wildly in the darkness, groping for and slapping his wrists. He momentarily lost his grip on her throat, allowing Catherine to draw in a deep breath that burned her heaving lungs. She tried to scream again, but the airman killed her cry with thumbs that dug deep into her windpipe. Catherine bucked and thrashed her body. The airman's grip, however, did not falter, and the crushing weight on her stomach remained steady. The airman made no sound until Catherine managed—with a monumental effort of strength and dexterity—to drive a booted foot into his gut. The airman tumbled off the bed and crashed headfirst onto the floor with a yelp. Catherine leapt to her feet and jumped over the airman's sprawled form. Her assailant scrambled forward and frantically grabbed for her ankle. He missed and tripped, hitting the floor with a bruising thump.

"Murder! Police!" Catherine yelled, fleeing the apartment. She charged into the hallway and banged on the door of the flat opposite, where Kitty McQuillen—a barmaid at the Duke of York on Victoria Street—had just settled down for a cup of tea. The time was 11 p.m. Kitty, surprised by the commotion outside her door, was even more startled when she opened it and found her neighbor standing there in nothing but boots and a necklace.

"Please, let me in!" Catherine screamed. "Save me, please! This man is trying to kill me!"

Over Catherine's shoulder, Kitty could see her neighbor's door was open and that the flat beyond was in darkness. Ambient light cast by a bulb in the hallway revealed the faint outline of a man standing in Catherine's room. Kitty could see the man had no clothes on, but the opening of another door at the end of the hallway momentarily distracted her attention. An elderly woman stuck her head out and demanded to know the reason for the all the fuss. But one look at the shrieking naked woman outside Kitty McQuillen's door satisfied her curiosity, and she quickly retreated back into the sanctity of her own place.

"Send for the police!" Catherine shrieked again, when the man in her flat suddenly spoke.

"Give me a light," he said. His voice was not threatening—it was, in fact, surprisingly calm, as if the strange episode unfolding was as normal as sitting down at the breakfast table to sip coffee.

Kitty let Catherine into her apartment and grabbed an empty flower vase that stood on a small side table just inside the doorway. There would be violent hell to pay if the man tried to enter her flat.

"Have you got a shilling for the electric light?" Catherine asked.

Kitty shook her head.

"Miss," the man's calm voice said from the darkness across the hall. "Give me a match."

A box of matches sat on the table from which Kitty had grabbed the vase. She reached for it and threw it into Catherine's apartment. Both women could see the man walk toward Catherine's open door. Kitty tightened her grip on the vase and raised it slightly in what she hoped was a menacing gesture. She could see the man bend down and pick the matches up. He struck one, revealing what Kitty thought was a very pointed chin and a wiry build.

"Have you seen my boots?" the airman called out to Catherine, who remained huddled close behind Kitty.

The two women watched from Kitty's doorway as the airman stumbled around in the dark of Catherine's room, trying to pick up his clothes. The match in his hand went out and he quickly struck another. All the while, he could be heard mumbling to himself, though the words were unintelligible. Somehow he managed to dress himself, and he moved to the doorway of Catherine's flat. Kitty raised the vase above her head and readied herself to attack. Catherine—breathing heavily—maintained a tight grip on Kitty's shoulder, her nails digging through the material of Kitty's shirt and leaving small crescent moons on her skin. The airman stepped into the hallway, and Catherine could now see he was quite unsteady, as if staggering out of a pub after a particularly bawdy binge. He continued to mumble to himself.

"You're a murderer!" Catherine yelled.

The airman offered no rebuttal to Catherine's accusation—he simply kept talking to himself and began fishing through his pockets for something.

"You're the one whose been killing the women around here!" Catherine shrieked.

The airman pulled his roll of paper money from his pocket. He counted out eight one-pound notes and threw them in Catherine's direction.

"I'm sorry," he said. "I think I had too much to drink this evening."

The two women watched him stumble down the stairs and exit through the building's main entrance. They stood where they were for several minutes in an attempt to reclaim their nerves. Where moments before there had been the sound of Catherine's mad shrieking and the apologetic tones of the airman, there was now only the sound of the two women's heavy breathing.

FEBRUARY 13, 1942

TWELVE

Barbara Lowe would visit her mother, Margaret, every third week. The visits always followed the same routine. The fifteen-year-old would take a Friday afternoon train from Southend up to London and arrive at her mother's flat at about 4:30 p.m. She would spend the weekend, during which mother and daughter might see a movie or walk through Hyde Park and Kensington Gardens. Sometimes they would go shopping. Come Sunday, Barbara would leave her mother's at 6:30 p.m. and take the train back to Southend, for she had to be back in time for Monday morning classes at St. Gabriel's. Such a schedule might seem too much to cope with for one so young, but Barbara—like other wartime children—had been forced to mature quickly.

Margaret had been an absentee mother even before she moved to London and left her daughter at boarding school. In November 1940, eight years after her husband's death, Margaret moved herself and her daughter into a property called Windmere Lodge on Southend Road. The intent had been to take in lodgers and make a living by running a guest-house. The business, however, proved a failure, prompting Margaret to make weekly sojourns into London to make money. She would leave on a Monday and return on Friday, leaving young Barbara by herself to care for the lodge. Although such an arrangement appears callous, the war put families under great pressure and made unfair demands, sometimes costing children the luxury of childhood.

At 4:30 p.m. on Friday, February 13, Barbara arrived at her mother's address—Flat 4, 9/10 Gosfield Street—wondering with much excitement what plans were in store for the next two days. She knocked on her mother's door and stood patiently with her travel case in hand, waiting for the door to open and Margaret's arms to wrap themselves around her in a warm greeting. Receiving no response, she knocked again and was met only by silence. Thinking her mother might have gone out shopping to buy food for dinner, Barbara left the building and walked down the road to 4 Gosfield Street. It was here she knew her mother had a friend, Mrs. Carleton, who lived in Flat 20. Barbara knocked on Mrs. Carleton's door in the hopes she might find out where her mother had gone. Mrs. Carleton told Barbara she hadn't seen Margaret in two or three days, nor could she offer any explanation as to where she might be. Leaving her travel case with her mother's friend, Barbara decided to take a short walk and then try back at her mother's flat.

She returned less than an hour later and knocked on the door again. This time, Barbara received a response, though it was not the one she expected. One of the neighbors opened his door and called to her in a gentle voice. His features were strained in an awkward smile—the kind one employs when trying to soften the delivery of what could be devastating news. Barbara recognized the man, but didn't know his name—she knew him only as "the Jewish gentleman." He invited her into his apartment, where two uniformed police officers were waiting. "Police officers informed me that a parcel had been left outside the flat for about two or three days," Barbara later said. "They wanted to get into the apartment."

Summoned by the officers, Detective Sergeant Leonard Blacktop—assigned to the Tottenham Court Police Station— had arrived at 9/10 Gosfield Street minutes later. His inquiries led him to the apartment of Mrs. Carleton, who had a spare set of keys to Margaret Lowe's flat. He entered Margaret's home and moved cautiously along the inside passage, into the kitchen. The room was blacked out, but light from the passageway illuminated a closed door on the other side of the room. Blacktop moved through the kitchen and tried opening the door. It was locked. He knocked and got no answer. He searched the flat—going through cupboards and drawers—looking for a key. When his search proved futile, he forced the door open with a well-placed kick and found the room in pitch blackness.

He felt along the wall for the light and turned it on. His attention was immediately drawn to the bed on the right side of the room. Margaret Lowe's head protruded from the sheets. The bed clothing covered her body and had been pulled up under her chin. A pillowcase obscured her face. Blacktop approached the bed, pulled the sheets back and brushed aside the pillowcase. A tight ligature had been tied around the woman's neck. A white, frothy substance bubbled from her nose and mouth. Her head looked to the left, and her face felt cold. Blacktop called to one of the uniformed officers standing outside the apartment and instructed him to summon senior police officers and the divisional police surgeon.

There had been no gruesome discovery on Wednesday, February 11. Likewise, Thursday passed without Greeno or Cherrill being summoned to the scene of another grisly mutilation. Over the course of those two days, a terrible air of expectancy taunted the two investigators. Every telephone ring carried with it the potential for news of further carnage in the West End. There was no reason to think the murderer had ceased his bloody rampage. He had struck on Sunday, Monday and Tuesday. This sudden break in violence, however, offered some small relief for detectives who found themselves confounded by a killer who worked at an unrelenting clip. Investigators used the respite to again question the families of Hamilton and Oatley and review their backgrounds for any common link. There appeared to be none, and the killings seemed as random as a roll of the dice. Greeno's curiosity, meanwhile, was piqued by this unexpected change in pace. Had the man he sought been arrested for an unrelated crime or killed while crossing the street? Perhaps the killer was a member of the military and had shipped out to a foreign battlefield—or maybe the latest victim was lying somewhere, rotting, and had yet to be discovered. The detectives had little time to ponder which theory was the correct one, for they soon found out, when the telephone on Greeno's desk rang early Friday evening.

The two investigators—along with Detective Sergeant Alexander Findlay—arrived at the Gosfield Street crime scene at 6:30 p.m. The apartment was on the building's ground floor, its layout simple: There was a sitting room in the front, a bedroom in the back and a passageway leading to a cramped kitchen. One door in the kitchen opened up to a small enclosed balcony and restroom. As Cherrill hunted for prints, Greeno inspected the body. Although the woman's head could be seen above the bedclothes, her body lay hidden beneath a black eiderdown. The detectives entering the room found the atmosphere unnaturally still, despite harboring the knowledge of what lay beneath the blankets.

The bedroom's furnishings were scarce. A night table, a chair and a rug did little to complement the ratty bed. Alexander Baldie, the divisional police surgeon, had already arrived on the scene. He told Greeno that judging from the temperature of the woman's neck, she had been killed sometime in the early morning hours. Her face looked livid, and the froth around her nose and mouth was tinged slightly pink. The ligature around her neck had been tied in a knot just under the right angle of her jaw. Beneath the black eiderdown were three blankets and one sheet. Greeno carefully turned the top bedclothes down and exposed the naked body underneath. The woman lay on her back. Her legs were wide apart, and her knees were bent and drawn up. She had suffered a severe mutilation. The killer had worked himself into a frenzy and surpassed the barbarity of Evelyn Oatley's murder. Her abdomen had been torn open, the skin ripped apart in a five-inch gash that exposed the intestines and other internal organs. On the right side of her groin was, noted Greeno, "a deep, gaping wound about ten inches long." Blood had flowed heavily from this dissection, forming a thick, congealed pool on the bedsheets between her legs. Another deep cut in the woman's pubic hair ran just above her vagina in a jagged line. A bloodstained wax candle had been pushed up inside of her.

Just below the wound to the right side of the victim's

groin was a large, blue-handled bread knife, its saw-edged blade—caked in a thick layer of blood—pointed inward and downward. A black-handled table knife—its blade noticeably worn down and smeared with blood—also lay across her thigh, pointing upward and outward. Lying close to her vagina was a yellow-handled table knife with its bloodstained blade resting on the bedsheets. Next to this knife was a small vegetable knife. Its blade, too, stained crimson, pointed inward and downward. Between the woman's legs—lying horizontally across the bed—lay a metal poker, the handle of which had been broken off. The metal at the break appeared to be new. After making notes of his observations, Greeno ordered one of the uniformed officers to summon Sir Bernard Spilsbury.

Cherrill, meanwhile, busied himself searching for prints. He had no doubt the killer would prove to be left-handed. The woman's clothing—a coat, sweater and skirt—lay in a messy pile at the foot of the bed, as if removed in a hurry. A hat with a feather lay on the floor beside the bed. Next to the hat was a solitary stocking that appeared to match the one tied around the woman's neck. After observing the body, Cherrill's attention came to bear on a glass candleholder on the bedroom's mantelpiece. He approached with magnifying glass in hand and found prints on the holder's base. In the well of the holder were small pieces of wax the same color as the candle protruding from between the victim's legs. On the right side of the mantelpiece sat a tumbler containing what looked like beer. Passing his magnifying glass over the tumbler's surface, Cherrill made note of several more prints and returned his attention to the candlestick holder. He again examined the prints at its base and determined that the fingers of a right hand had made them. The fingerprint man imagined himself as the killer and made as if he were removing the candle from the holder. It was apparent from his exercise that a right-handed person would place his left hand at the base of the holder. Alternately, a left-handed person would place his right hand at the holder's base. Cherrill ordered that both the glass and the holder be secured for transportation back to the Yard. He continued combing the apartment, looking for more prints, and found a bottle of beer on a small table in the kitchen. The label on the bottle read, "Hammerton's Oatmeal Stout." The bottle was about one-third full and also bore finger marks. Cherrill ordered that this be bagged as evidence along with the other items.

Spilsbury arrived at the flat at 8:30 p.m. to conduct a closer examination of the body. He noted that the victim's pupils were dilated and that blood was present beneath the surface of the whites. Her hair was caught under the ligature around her neck. Above the stocking, her face appeared flushed and her nostrils were clogged with blood and mucus. Spilsbury removed a male contraceptive from a pool of drying blood lying near the victim's crotch. It was extended, bloodstained, and appeared used. It was bagged as evidence. Using an electric torch to better illuminate the carnage, Spilsbury studied the wounds to the woman's abdomen and thigh. The candle had been pushed about six inches up into her vagina. With a gloved hand, Spilsbury removed the violation. The candle, although caked in blood, looked knew. It was put in a container and given to Cherrill. The pathologist worked in silence, while Greeno stood back and watched. After about half an hour, Spilsbury turned to the detective and said that from his cursory examination it appeared the cause of death was manual strangulation. Greeno nodded and ordered that the body be removed to the Paddington Mortuary.

Greeno resumed his search of the apartment while

Spilsbury supervised the removal of the body. On the mantelpiece, near where the candlestick holder and tumbler
had been found, Greeno found the missing half of the broken poker. This he collected as evidence. A broken clock,
its hands stopped at 3:40, lay on its side under the bed. On
the kitchen table were some letters and three ration books
in the name of Margaret Lowe. Nearby were a lipstick
case, an electric torch and two Yale-pattern keys, which
proved to fit the front door to Margaret's flat and the street
entrance to the building. On the floor, near the table and
wedged between a wooden tub and a cardboard carton, was
Margaret's black handbag. It was open about an inch. Lying across the top of the bag were two folded one-pound
notes. Greeno made note of the serial numbers: M. 14D.
046046 and J. 49D. 20750. Inside the bag was a pouch
with two more folded pound notes in it. Greeno also made
note of these serial numbers and ordered Findlay to run a
trace on them. Also in the bag was a woman's white handkerchief, two crushed cigarettes, a stamp and a gramo-
phone needle tin. In the tin were seven and a half pills: Two
were white, one was blue, and the other four and a half
were pink. The bag and its contents were collected as evidence. Greeno noted that the bag had been hidden from
view, which probably accounted for why the money had
not been taken as it had at the Hamilton and Oatley murder
scenes. The larder cupboard in the kitchen was open, and
the cutlery inside had been rifled through. From this selection of silverware, the killer had picked his arsenal.

Cherrill returned to Scotland Yard just after 8:30 p.m.
Tired but determined, he began his examination of the
evidence taken from Margaret Lowe's flat. He dusted and

removed the prints from the candlestick holder and the tumbler. He opted not to compare these latest prints with those from the Hamilton and Oatley murder scenes. He felt confident the impressions from all three scenes were left by the same man—but not the same fingers. Instead, Cherrill searched the Yard's fingerprint catalog for a match. As with his recent excursions through the records, the search turned up nothing. The sense of disappointment was strangely levied by the adrenaline surge that came from knowing a serial killer was on the loose. He pinched the bridge of his nose in thoughtful contemplation. Exhaustion had crept up on him and was urging him home. Never one to argue with good advice, Cherrill had just put on his coat and was reaching for his hat when the phone on his desk rang.

"Fingerprint office," he said, noting the flat tone of his own voice. Looking at the clock humming on the wall, he saw that it was closing in on 11 p.m.

"Another woman's been found murdered," Greeno's voice said down the line, "Sussex Gardens, Paddington."

Henry Jouannet had sensed something wrong.

At 7 p.m. on Friday the 13th, he returned home from work to have dinner with Doris as his daily routine dictated. The morning's milk delivery still stood on the doorstep. He picked up the pint bottle and unlocked the front door, calling out his wife's name. There was no reply. He walked along a small passageway and entered the apartment's large front room. The blackout curtains were drawn and the room was dark. He turned on the light and saw the remains of the previous night's meal—several biscuits and a jug of milk—still sitting on the table. Something slithered across his guts and skittered up his spine as he called his wife's name again. Silence settled on his shoulders like a cold, sodden blanket. He walked back down the front passageway to their bedroom door, which he found locked. He knocked on the door and called through it to Doris. Nothing. His knocking quickly became a frantic pounding. Dropping to his hands and knees, he tried to peer under the door to get some idea of what catastrophe lay beyond. Although he could make out nothing specific, it was clear the bedroom light was on.

Henry leapt to his feet and ran down the hall to the bathroom. He yanked open drawers and rummaged through the medicine cabinet, hoping to find something with which to jimmy the bedroom door open. He charged into the kitchen when the bathroom failed to yield anything useful. Turning on the light, he stopped mid-stride. In the sink, still unwashed, were the two soup bowls—along with the spoons and knives—from last night's supper. Doris never procrastinated when it came to housework. She must have immediately gone out after seeing him off at the station the night before. A panicked scream for help rose in his throat as he ran to the building next door, at 189 Sussex Gardens. It was here their housekeeper, Mrs. Kirby, lived. She answered the heavy knocking at her door and found her employer in an agonized state.

"Have you seen my wife?" Henry asked. "Have you seen Doris?"

"No, Mr. Jouannet, I haven't seen her all day," Mrs. Kirby said, "and I noticed the front shutters in the sitting room have been closed all day."

"Come with me," Henry said. "I think something is wrong."

The two of them ran back to the apartment and the locked bedroom door. Henry tried keys to other rooms in the flat at Mrs. Kirby's suggestion, hoping one would fit the bedroom lock—none, however, did.

"I think we should call the police," Henry said.

Mrs. Kirby ran to a neighbor's flat and dialed the police. Henry stood anxiously outside and awaited their arrival.

Police Constable William Payne—responding from the Paddington Police Station—arrived at the Sussex Gardens address at 7:31 p.m. and was led to the locked bedroom door by a distraught Henry Jouannet. Payne asked Henry if the room had a window. Henry said it did, one that looked out to the rear of the building. Payne walked outside and cut through a side alley that led to the back of the address. He worked his way through some bushes and came to the window, which was shuttered and locked from the inside. Seeing no other alternative, he went back inside and told Henry the door would have to be forced open. With a hard kick, he partially dislodged the door from its hinges. The room beyond was not entirely dark, for a small electric fire in the middle of the far wall cast a pallid red glow onto the floor. A disarranged pillow sat on a chair in front of the fireplace. Payne turned to Henry and told him to stay where he was.

The constable entered the room and turned on the light. Against the left wall were two twin beds pushed together side by side. An ominous lump lay beneath the sheets of one of them. Payne approached the bed, again warning Henry not to enter. Bracing himself for what lay beneath, he pulled the bedclothes slightly down to reveal Doris Jouannet's lifeless face. He yanked the sheets back to expose a body—naked, except for a black, open nightgown— lying diagonally across the bed. The right arm pointed away from the torso. The left arm was situated so that the hand rested between the woman's legs. A stocking had been tightly bound around her neck, and the flesh beneath her left breast had been carved away. Her genitals had been stabbed and slashed. The woman's clothing was piled haphazardly on a chair at the foot of the bed. An empty condom sheath had been discarded on the floor. Nearby was a small nightstand on which sat a clock with its hands stopped at eight o'clock. Next to the clock was an ashtray, with the butt of a Craven "A" cigarette in it. On the south wall was the window Payne had tried to enter from outside. A large wardrobe rested against the wall opposite the window. At the wardrobe's base were two empty condom wrappers. A hand basin stood in the southwest corner of the room. Payne left the bedroom and found Henry—a live wire of nervous energy—pacing back and forth in the sitting room. He looked at Payne when the constable entered the room and knew from the policeman's solemn expression that Doris was dead.

"I must advise you not to go in that room," Payne said, before running to the flat next door to use the phone. At 7:50 p.m., Payne told his station officer to alert Scotland Yard's CID and the divisional surgeon.

Divisional Detective Leonard Clare—still investigating the killing of Evelyn Hamilton—responded to the murder scene at 8 p.m. He immediately made a survey of the premises and noted that 187 Sussex Gardens was a self-contained ground-floor flat, the only entrance to which was through a door off the street. Access to the other floors at No. 187 was actually gained through the building next door at No. 189, meaning that the Jouannets' flat was completely isolated from the other floors in the building.

The flat was spacious. All the rooms within were gained via a passageway that ran the flat's length. Constable Payne led Clare to the bedroom, where the inspector made his own observations. A pair of woman's slippers and two used condoms lay just inside the bedroom door. On a table in the northwest corner of the room was a Gillette pattern safety razor. An issue of the *Evening Standard,* dated February 12, lay on the floor at the foot of the bed. Another empty condom wrapper had been placed on top of the newspaper. Clare ordered that the woman's clothes on the nearby chair be collected as evidence. He leaned over the body and took note of the slash beneath the left breast and the wounds to the genitals. The bedsheets were soaked with blood. Ten minutes after Clare's arrival, the divisional surgeon, Dr. W. A. Kennedy, showed up with his little black bag in hand. He examined the body and quickly pronounced "life extinct."

His night already busy, Greeno—accompanied by Sergeant Alexander Findlay—did not arrive at Sussex Gardens until 10:30 p.m. He came directly from Gosfield Street, having been alerted to this latest act of butchery by a motorcycle messenger dispatched by the Yard. The body had not been disturbed. Her complexion was pale and her hair was fair. She had a slender face and a very thin body. For a woman she had been quite tall, and Greeno estimated her height to be nearly six feet. The stocking around her neck was made of silk and had been tied in a knot just under her chin and slightly to the left. Skin had been scraped away from her right cheek, leaving a bloody mark. The wound beneath the left breast measured about four inches long. Perpendicular to this, a deep gash nearly six inches in length ran down the midline of the stomach, from below the navel to just above the vaginal entrance. A six-inch cut to the left of the groin had flowed heavily onto the sheets. A clean-cut wound about half an inch in length to the right side of the victim's left nipple violated the skin. "The manner in which this wound was inflicted," noted Greeno, "suggests that it was cut by an instrument held in the left hand."

A stocking that matched the one around her neck lay across the woman's right leg. Greeno walked to the table in the northwest corner of the room and examined the Gillette safety razor. Manufactured by Kingsway, the blade was stained with blood. There was a nail file, a pair of manicure scissors and a cuticle stick. A thin layer of dust covered the table's surface except in two spots, stretching from the base of the mirror to the edge of the drawer cabinet. One of the clean areas measured one and one-eighth inches wide; the other measured about a quarter of an inch wide, suggesting that two items had recently been taken from the table. Also on the table was a small, light-colored purse, inside of which Greeno found a Yale-pattern house key adhered to a piece of tape and secured to the purse's inner lining with a safety pin. He gave the key to Findlay, who determined that the key opened the front door to the flat. The purse also contained some loose change and a few white pills. It looked to Greeno like someone had already rifled through its contents.

In one of the dressing table drawers, the inspector found a packet of Elastoplast dressing strip—some of which had been cut away. On the floor between the wardrobe and the bedroom door, Greeno spotted two condoms. One appeared used and contained fluid. A piece of tissue paper was screwed up nearby and was wet with some substance. Greeno ordered that the items be collected as evidence. In the wardrobe, Greeno found two handbags. One bag contained loose change; in the other was a Gillette-pattern safety razor, the same as that found on the dressing table. Greeno stepped into the middle of the room and took in everything. If the murders continued at this unabated pace, a public panic would soon ensue. The war and the city's position on the front line aside, the thought of a serial killer actively stalking the blacked-out streets would strike many as a more immediate threat than the Luftwaffe. Greeno examined the empty bed. At first glance, it appeared to be undisturbed, but—upon closer inspection—he noticed a stain on the corner of one of the sheets. He pulled the sheet back and saw that the underside was wet with blood. By now, Spilsbury had arrived and was on bent knees examining the body. He told Greeno to have the sheets bagged and sent to the police laboratory in Hendon, North London, for examination.

The recently arrived Cherrill, meanwhile, conducted his own study of the premises. He thought it immediately apparent that whoever had butchered Evelyn Oatley and Margaret Lowe had also slaughtered Doris Jouannet. The mutilations were strikingly similar, and the barbarity of all three murders was such that one would be hard-pressed to believe multiple killers of such ferocity were operating simultaneously within the same limited confines of the city. All the killings had occurred within a two-mile radius of one another. As at the other murder scenes, here there appeared to be no sign of a struggle. Cherrill swept every inch of the room with his magnifying glass. On a hand mirror lying on the dressing table, he found a cluster of prints. Their quality was questionable and, in all likelihood, belonged to the victim—regardless, he ordered that it be sent to his office. Numerous prints were found on the bedroom door and the doors of the wardrobe. Cherrill ordered that the bedroom and wardrobe doors be removed and taken to the Yard for further examination.

The hunt continued.

THIRTEEN

He was not immune to the grim nature of his work. The mutilation of children and violent murder in its infinite forms was slowly corroding Sir Bernard Spilsbury's spirit. There was a constant air of melancholy about him. Inside, he carried the heavy weight of depression, which would lead him to take his own life two years after the war. Others in his line of work—and the detectives he associated with—responded to the gruesome nature of their profession with a dark sense of humor. It was a defense mechanism, a means to deflect the burden of constantly baring witness to the product of man's behavior at its most vile. But Spilsbury found no humor—grim or otherwise—in what he did. Each case weighed painfully on his psyche. The March 11, 1935, issue of *Time* magazine referred to Spilsbury as "His Majesty's Government's real-life Sherlock Holmes," but Spilsbury was far more human than the great fictional sleuth, and the cases he handled were of a much bloodier nature.

Nevertheless, his name was as much a part of the English murder industry as any great literary detective—and when a case came along that thwarted even Spilsbury's knowledge of death, the press took note. As *Time* magazine pointed out in its article, the great pathologist was "famously foiled" in the 1934 Brighton Trunk Murders, a case that garnered sensational coverage for the day. One summer afternoon that year, a pervasively musty odor settled over the seaside town's railway station. The stench was overwhelming and was noticed by all who were disembarking and boarding the trains. The source of the smell was found in the station's baggage room, emanating from a trunk, which apparently contained the limbless torso of a woman. As *Time* reported, here "was a case for Sir Bernard Spilsbury." But even Spilsbury's forensic expertise failed to secure a conviction in the case, and the murder went officially unsolved despite the arrest of a suspect. The burden each murder placed on Spilsbury, and the gory nature of his work, grew even more cumbersome as time went by. The death of his two sons during the war only added to the trauma, but he persisted with the tasks he was presented. For Spilsbury, there was nothing to laugh about.

Greeno arrived at the Paddington Mortuary at 2:30 p.m. on Saturday. The pathologist was already there in his leather apron, arranging sharp instruments on a metal tray. Greeno handed Spilsbury the two condoms he had found on the floor of Doris Jouannet's bedroom the previous evening, along with the piece of crumpled tissue that appeared to be soiled by some fluid that would most likely prove to be semen. Spilsbury put the items aside for later analysis and continued with his prep work for the pending autopsy. He didn't speak as he readied himself for the task ahead. Over the years, repetition had done nothing to decrease for him the morbidity of cutting open the dead. Greeno watched in silence as Spilsbury wheeled the Jouannet woman's body into position. The time had come for the dead to speak.

The stocking was still tied around her throat, with the knot situated one inch in front of the angle of the left jaw. Carefully, Spilsbury untied the knot and removed the stocking. He laid it out alongside the body and measured it, noting its length at ten and a half inches. A pale pressure mark was visible on the skin where the stocking had been, measuring three-quarters of an inch wide and encircling the entire neck. Her face was livid, and tiny hemorrhages were present in her upper-left eyelid and the whites of her eyes. Spilsbury studied the abrasion on the woman's right cheek. He turned her head slightly toward him and inspected a number of scratches on the left side of her face. Spilsbury told Greeno they were more than likely left by fingernails—possibly inflicted as the woman shook her head in violent protest as she fought for her life. Around the inner side of the woman's left nipple was a clean cut, measuring half an inch long. There was no blood in the wound, which had partly separated the nipple and was inflicted by a knife moving in an outward direction away from the center of the breast.

There was a four-inch gash that curved along the lower part of the left breast. Upon more minute examination, Spilsbury noticed that the wound was actually two deep knife cuts that merged into one. The woman's naval had been violently dissected. The gash started one inch below the navel and extended five and a half inches downward. It cut through the lower part of the abdominal wall. The skin of the abdomen was beginning to turn green, indicating the onset of decomposition. The killer had exercised a certain restraint until he went to work on his victim below the naval. A slash measuring nearly three inches passed through the pubic region and along the left side of the vaginal entrance. Extending from the woman's left thigh, a six-inch gash cut through the pallid skin and stopped just short of the vagina. The wound was deep and filled with blood.

"It's this wound that accounts for the blood found on her dressing gown," Spilsbury said. "The other wounds had little or no blood in them."

A superficial wound ran parallel to the major cut and showed only minor signs of bleeding. No blood or seminal secretions were found in the woman's vagina, and despite damage to the surrounding area, the genitals were free of injury. The external examination done, Spilsbury reached for his scalpel and began to cut. Internally, there were numerous small hemorrhages in the lining of the scalp and at the front of the head. The body's organs appeared healthy but were congested with blood. There was evidence of hemorrhaging on the surface of the heart, which was slightly enlarged. The tonsils, Spilsbury noted, were thick with blood. The body contained some partly digested food, which Spilsbury determined were the remnants of the final dinner Doris Jouannet ate with her husband. Having completed his examination, Spilsbury turned to Greeno.

"In my opinion, the cause of death was strangulation by the ligature around the neck," he said. "The other injuries could have been caused by a razor blade like the one found in the flat."

He looked over the body again and pointed to the neck.

"The act of strangulation came first, I think," he said. "Because of the blood present, the wound in the left thigh was caused immediately after. The wound around the left breast was inflicted at the point of death. The lack of bleeding in the other wounds suggests they were made after death."

Greeno nodded and watched as Spilsbury covered Doris Jouannet's corpse with a blanket. Henry Jouannet had identified his wife's body in the morgue earlier that morning. He suspected his wife had returned to her old way of life, but he had never wanted to admit it to himself. To do so, he thought, was to acknowledge a certain failure on his part. But he had done all he could. His body tensed when the gurney was wheeled out and the blanket pulled down. He stifled a small cry in his throat and nodded before slowly turning away.

The autopsy results of Doris Jouannet had been startlingly similar to those of Margaret Lowe, whose body had gone under Spilsbury's blade at 11:20 that morning at the Paddington Mortuary. As in the case of Jouannet, a stocking measuring nearly eleven inches in length had been removed from Lowe's neck. The ligature had been tied so tightly that it left a permanent bruise around the woman's neck. Her nose was heavily clogged with blood and mucus, and her mouth was filled with pink, frothy sputum—some of which had dribbled down her chin. There was blood beneath the whites of her eyes and hemorrhages in her eyelids. Unlike the other bodies, Lowe's showed evidence of having been battered before the life was slashed and strangled from her.

A dark bruise along the lower left jaw and another on the outer side of the left shoulder were clearly visible. A blue and purple bruise had discolored the skin over her left knee, and two smaller bruises were evident just above her right shin. There was a severe bruise on the back of her head on the left side. Another bruise—this one not as dark in color—covered the right temple. There were two bruises over each lower jaw. Then there were the knife wounds. A deep gash, five inches long, had opened the skin of her abdomen, penetrating the peritoneal cavity and exposing the small intestine. The woman's uterus had also been slashed. Along the lengthy gash there were five small superficial wounds, none of which appeared to have bled. Another five cuts extended out from the pubic region and stretched behind the orifice of the vagina. These wounds had only bled a little. A ten-inch cut defaced the skin of the right thigh.

The internal organs were congested, and her airways were packed with blood and mucus. Hemorrhaging was present in the lining of the larynx. Spilsbury opened the woman's mouth and examined the tongue, which showed slight bruising at the tip. Her stomach was empty, except for a small amount of fluids. There was no seminal fluid or blood in the vagina. The woman's uterus appeared greatly enlarged and contained a number of fibroid tumors.

As in the case of Doris Jouannet, the cause of death for Margaret Lowe was strangulation by a ligature.

"From the bruises, I think she was knocked down first," Spilsbury told Greeno. "She knocked her head hard and was then strangled. The wound to the right thigh was inflicted immediately after strangulation. The cuts to the genitals were made at the point of death. The wound to the abdomen was made after death. The wounds could have been caused by any of the knives found on the body."

It was Spilsbury's opinion that the white-handled vegetable knife found lying near the woman's groin had been used to inflict the majority of the carnage. Of all the knives recovered at the scene, this one had the sharpest blade.

Greeno now had four bodies on his hands and no suspect. Little did he know, developments in a case seemingly unrelated to the butchering of four women would soon give him the suspect he so desperately sought.

While Spilsbury was applying scalpel to flesh, Frederick Cherrill busied himself with the items removed from the Jouannet crime scene. The majority of impressions lifted from the bedroom and wardrobe doors were smudged, but there were a few that could possibly point investigators toward an apprehension. When he worked, Cherrill often pondered a particular passage from the Bible. The musing had little to do with religious beliefs and more to do with the endless fascination he harbored for his job. The passage was Job 37:7: "He sealeth up the hand of every man; that all men may know his work."

There were some who believed the Job passage referred directly to the ancient use of fingerprints, but Cherrill was not one of them. He believed that fingerprints were an unintentional component in the creation of man—much like some flaw in a work of art. Cherrill argued that ancient people were wholly ignorant as to the existence of fingerprints. To support his thesis, he often referred to the murder of Jezebel at the behest of Jehu in chapter nine of the second Book of Kings. Had the murder taken place in 1940s London, the killer would have undoubtedly been brought to justice. The biblical crime scene is described in verses twenty-five through twenty-seven: "And when he was come in, he did eat and drink, and said, Go, see now this cursed woman, and bury her: for she is a king's daughter. And they went to bury her: but they found no more of her than the skull, and the feet, and the palms of her hands."

"The palms of her hands" are all any worthwhile investigator would need to identify the body. If fingerprinting did exist back then, Cherrill often argued, surely the killer would have known this and destroyed the hands. All this and more passed through Cherrill's head as he meticulously dusted the bedroom and wardrobe doors, lifting what prints he could. Before turning to the Yard's cataloged index, he compared the latents to prints taken from Doris Jouannet in the morgue earlier that day. This step brought his hunt to a quick end, for the prints he was able to lift were those of the victim—as were those taken from the hand mirror he had removed as evidence from the scene. Cherrill sat back down at his desk and ran a hand through his thinning crop of silver hair, not yet realizing that the man he hunted was already in police custody.

Gordon Cummins realized trouble had finally found him. It had gone 4 a.m. Friday morning by the time he decided to return to his billet. He would have to sneak into his quarters and enter his bunk room via the fire escape, as he usually did on nights he stayed out late. He was supposed to have reported back in by 10:30 the previous night, February 12. Saturday was the only night cadets were allowed to stay out late, not having to return to quarters until midnight. But his tardiness was the least of his worries on this particular predawn morning. Of more pressing concern was the fact that he had lost his respirator. He had been sitting at a bar, drinking whiskey late the previous night when it dawned on him he was no longer in possession of his issued gas mask. He knew retracing his steps in search of it was an impossibility, for such a course of action could leave him vulnerable to trouble far more serious than an RAF reprimand. He finished his drink and ordered another, pondering recent events. He decided he did not want his respirator to be found at the scene of something dubious. In his head, he quickly retraced his steps for the evening . . . Yes, that was it, the Captain's Club at St. James's Market!

He downed the remaining contents of his glass and scurried from the pub to where he had made an unsuccessful go at a good-night kiss. He still had the woman's phone number in his wallet. It did not take him long to find the scene of his failed amorous attempt—it took an even shorter amount of time to realize his respirator was no longer there. The question of where it was did not bother him as much as the question of who had it. Realizing that hanging about and dwelling on it served no purpose, he returned to Piccadilly Circus and ambled into a crowded pub. He took a seat at the bar beside another airman, making a point to avoid conversation. He drank several whiskeys and pondered the evening's unfortunate turn of events. Unfortunate, of course, was a far cry from disastrous, and he saw no reason why some quick thinking should not extricate him from his current circumstance. He had one more drink and dragged the back of his hand across his mouth. Making sure the other airman's attention was diverted elsewhere, he casually leaned down and picked up the man's respirator, which rested against the left leg of his bar stool.

Charles Johnson, the orderly sergeant at St. James's Close, had gone to check on Cummins at 1:30 a.m. and was annoyed to find the airman still out. He approached the sentries on duty and instructed them to notify him when Cummins returned. Three hours later, Commander Cook—the guard commander—called Johnson in the orderly sergeant's room to report that a sentry had caught Cummins trying to sneak back into his billet. Johnson asked that the delinquent airman be brought to him immediately, and he found himself standing face to face with Cummins ten minutes later.

"Where have you been?" Johnson asked him.

"I have been to a party," Cummins said.

"Where did you get that respirator from?"

Cummins eyed the thing dumbly.

"The civil police phoned here," Johnson said. "They have your respirator, and they want to talk to you."

"I have been pub drinking—someone must have picked up mine by mistake and I have his," Cummins said.

"Your respirator was found at the scene of a crime," Johnson said. "A woman was attacked in the West End."

"I told you that I was at a party, and then I went to a pub."

He ordered Cummins to his room to await the arrival of the civil authorities.

"Am I under arrest?" Cummins asked.

Johnson told him he wasn't and said he could return to his room without an armed escort, which he did. Back at his billet, Cummins fell heavily onto his bunk and sat on its edge with his head in his hands. He sighed deeply and studied the respirator next to him. The situation was critical. His mind raced frantically to find a plausible story or excuse he hoped might explain his way out of things, but nothing that sounded convincing materialized. In frustration, he knocked the respirator onto the floor and woke up the flight sergeant sleeping one bunk over.

"Where have you been?" the sergeant asked.

"I'm in the shit," Cummins said. "Someone swooped my respirator and the bloody thing's been found at the scene of a crime. I have to wait here now for the police to arrive."

The sergeant offered his condolences and drifted back to sleep, leaving Cummins alone to once again ponder his predicament. Wondering how long it would be before the police arrived, he decided to polish his boots and the buttons on his uniform to while away the time. Meanwhile, back in the orderly sergeant's room, Johnson had called the RAF Police to inform them that Cummins had returned to his quarters. The Civil Police were notified and Detective Constable Charles Bennett was dispatched to bring Cummins to the West End Central Police Station. Bennett, and a uniformed constable, reported to Corporal Johnson at 5:45 a.m. Johnson went to Flat 27 and found Cummins, still fully dressed in his uniform, lying on his bunk with his hands folded behind his head. He was not asleep and immediately leapt to his feet when Johnson called his name. Johnson told him the police were waiting for him and watched as Cummins fumbled for his gas mask. "He seemed to make an extra attempt to bring his respirator with him," Johnson later told authorities, "and in fact did take it." Cummins followed Johnson to the orderly sergeant's room, where Bennett sat waiting. From there, he was taken to the West End Central Police Station.

Bennett searched Cummins at the station and found a cigarette case in the left breast pocket of his RAF tunic. In another pocket, he found a leather wallet and a comb with missing teeth. Cummins—who remained silent—was then put in an interrogation room and left to await the arrival of Detective Sergeant Thomas Shepherd, who showed up at the station at 8 a.m. Once situated at his desk, Shepherd received from Bennett the cigarette case and the wallet. The detective sergeant immediately inventoried the wallet's contents and found a piece of paper with the assault victim's phone number—COL 6622—scribbled on it. There were several personal letters and some family snapshots, along with a Royal Air Force identity card bearing the name Gordon Frederick Cummins and his photograph. Also in the wallet's folds were several stamps and two one-pound Bank of England notes, Nos. J. 10.D. 453632 and L. 65.D. 765461. Shepherd next examined the respirator Cummins had in his possession. Inside the front flap of the carrying case were a metal wristwatch on a brown leather strap secured with strips of Elastoplast, and eight one-pound Bank of England notes. Shepherd made note of the bills' serial numbers then put all the seized property into his locker.

The clock on the wall said 9:30 when Shepherd sat down with Cummins. The airman appeared relaxed and offered a smile when Shepherd introduced himself and cautioned Cummins of his rights.

"You answer the description of an airman who assaulted a woman in St. Alban's Street, Haymarket, at about 9:45 p.m. last night," Shepherd said. "A service respirator with your regimental number on it was left behind by the person responsible."

"I have a hazy recollection of being with a woman," Cummins said cautiously. "I have been thinking it over, but I can't remember striking her. I would like to make a statement and tell you what I remember."

Shepherd nodded.

The story Cummins told was this:

"Last night, I was given the evening off and I booked out of Camp at about 6:30 p.m. Three other airmen were with me, and when we got to Baker Street, two of them went to the pictures, and a corporal and myself went to a pub—the Volunteer Public House. I don't know the corporal's name, but I'd know him if I saw him."

According to Cummins, he and the unnamed corporal sat in the pub and drank three double whiskeys each before downgrading to several pints of bitter. They drank for an hour, waiting for the alcohol to take hold before opting to venture over to the Trocadero. They left the pub and took a taxi to Shaftesbury Avenue, where they spent about twenty minutes drinking rye highballs at the Trocadero's bar.

"It was my friend who suggested going to the Universelle Brasserie," Cummins said. "When we arrived at the Brasserie, we went to the beer counter and had two half-pints of beer each. My friend was talking to another airman, so I left him and went over to the spirit bar. I had several whiskeys and brandies—I cannot remember how many, but I know it was several. After some minutes, I cannot remember how many exactly, I went over and spoke to a woman who was standing at the bottom of the stairs."

Cummins said he engaged the woman in friendly conversation, and the two of them grabbed a table and ordered a round of drinks. By this point, according to the airman, he had long left sobriety behind, and the exact details of their conversation and what happened afterward were lost in a haze of drink.

"I cannot remember exactly what followed," Cummins said. "I have a hazy recollection of walking round the streets with her. By this time, I was very drunk and did not know what I was doing."

Cummins told Shepherd the next clear recollection he had was of standing at Marble Arch at two-thirty in the morning with the realization that he had violated curfew.

"I remembered that I should be back at my depot," he said. "I caught a cab and went to Regent's Park."

"You remember nothing more about the evening?" Shepherd asked.

Cummins shook his head.

"I don't remember what happened after I left the restaurant with the woman," he said. "I certainly don't remember leaving her. I deeply regret what has happened and I am willing to pay her compensation."

"Did the woman give you her telephone number?" Shepherd asked.

Cummins creased his forehead in a display of mock concentration. He nodded slowly.

"Yes," he said. "I remember that when I spoke to her in the Brasserie, I asked her whether I could see her again. I think she gave me a piece of paper with her telephone number on it. I don't remember what I did with the paper, but I think I screwed it up and put it in my pocket."

As Cummins spoke, Shepherd scribbled in his notebook. The airman delivered his version of events in a cool, unshaken manner. He smiled apologetically throughout the story and lent a remorseful tone to his voice. He told Shepherd he was married and had recently been accepted into the RAF's pilot-training program. Shepherd nodded, doubting Cummins would ever see the inside of an airplane again.

"Will you please write down what you just told me?" Shepherd said, sliding a pad and pen across the table.

"Certainly," Cummins said and took the pen in his left hand. When he finished writing his statement, he signed it, dated it and pushed the pad back across the table.

Shepherd read it over. Cummins sat silently in his chair with his hands flat on the table in front of him. The knuckles of the middle two fingers on his left hand were cut and freshly scabbed over.

"How did you hurt your hand?" Shepherd asked.

Cummins looked casually at the wounds. "I was working on an airplane engine some time ago and banged my fingers," he said. "Because of the cold weather, they've taken a while to heal."

Shepherd, not believing the airman's explanation, made a note of the wounds.

"I'm arresting you and charging you with assault," he told Cummins in a matter-of-fact voice before advising the airman of his rights.

Cummins sat motionless and offered no reply.

Meanwhile, at 29 Southwick Street, Catherine Mulcahy sat on a chair in her small flat and sucked nervously on a cigarette. Divisional Detective Inspector Leonard Clare sat opposite her and listened as she detailed—between long drags on her smoke—her recent assault at the hands of an English airman. She told Clare she believed her attacker was responsible for the recent murders in the West End— and that when she yelled this to the airman, he did nothing to refute the accusation.

"Can you describe him?" asked Clare, who had taken an immediate interest in Mulcahy's report when she filed it with the police earlier that morning.

"It was dark, and I didn't see his face properly," Catherine said. "I think if I came face to face with him I could recognize him. He would be about five feet, eight inches or five feet, nine inches, medium build—a wiry type of body. He said he was thirty-one. He was very well spoken and clean-shaven. He had greenish-gray eyes—what I mean by this is that they were very pale and gave me the impression he had been wearing glasses."

She told Clare the man had apologized for his behavior and thrown money at her as he left.

"He ended up giving me ten pounds," she said. "But he didn't actually have intercourse with me."

"Do you have that money?" Clare asked.

"I made fourteen pounds that night," she said, "all in one-pound notes."

She went to the small kitchenette area of her flat and retrieved the cash from a hiding place beneath the sink. She handed the wad of paper notes to Clare.

"The ten ones he gave me are in with these fourteen," she said.

Clare informed her that the money was now evidence in a police investigation. He gave her a receipt for the cash and told her the Metropolitan Police Department would reimburse her for the money, which it did the following day. Back at his office, Clare made a record of the serial numbers on the notes and booked the cash as evidence.

News of Cummins's apprehension had been a source of much excitement for those investigating the recent murders. Clare was convinced Cummins had killed Evelyn Hamilton in the surface air-raid shelter on Montague Place. That crime, although only a few days old, now seemed an eternity away as so much had transpired since that early Monday morning. Hamilton had been strangled. An airman—most likely Cummins—had tried to choke Mulcahy and the Heywood woman to death. At that first crime scene, Clare had ordered that mortar samples from the shelter be taken as evidence. Now, he wondered if they might not prove useful. He knew the police were in possession of Cummins's respirator. The detective theorized that Cummins would have placed his respirator on the ground of the air-raid shelter in order to finish off Hamilton—just as he had placed it on the ground when he attacked Mary Heywood in the doorway off St. James's Market. Clare reached for his phone and called Shepherd. He wanted to examine that respirator for himself.

FOURTEEN

After witnessing the autopsies of Margaret Lowe and Doris Jouannet, Greeno returned to his office at the Tottenham Court Road Police Station and received word of Cummins's arrest. He ordered copies of Mary Heywood's statement relating to her assault the night before, and Cummins's written account in which he provided his own blurred version of events. Also made available for Greeno's review was the transcribed statement of Catherine Mulcahy. The fact that choking seemed to be the suspect's preferred method of attack intrigued Greeno, just as it had Clare, for all four murder victims had either been strangled or violently choked. Presently, Greeno sat back in his chair and allowed himself a tired smile. At last, the investigation had a strong focal point.

Detective Tom Shepherd drove to St. James's Close, Regent's Park, at 8:20 p.m. to inspect Cummins's living quarters. He met with the corporal in charge, who led him to Room B and its eight bunks in Flat 27. The corporal pointed out Cummins's bunk in the center of the room. A kit bag sat on top of the covers. Hanging on the top-left bedpost was an airman's jacket. Shepherd rifled through the jacket and found in the right-hand breast pocket a black fountain pen with a gold band encircling the cap. The initials "D.J." were engraved in the gold. Aware that the body of one Doris Jouannet had been discovered the night before, Shepherd took the pen as evidence.

The detective opened the kit bag and pulled out a crumpled shirt. A small, well-defined red spot on the inner side of the collar near the right buttonhole immediately seized his attention. There was another red stain on the front of the shirt near the third buttonhole, and further red staining on the outer side of the left cuff. More stains were found on the inner surface of the shirt near the right shoulder. Along with the shirt, Shepherd found a white towel that had three small red stains on it. The shirt and towel were taken as evidence. Shepherd ordered they be sent—along with the shirt from the kit bag—to the police laboratory for examination. He returned to the West End Central Police Station and again confronted Cummins, this time showing him the initialed fountain pen he had found in Cummins's tunic. The airman played ignorant, telling Shepherd the pen did not belong to him and he was oblivious as to how it found its way into his pocket.

Greeno, meanwhile, wasted no time in pursuing his new lead. He traversed the city's darkened streets, asking working girls if they had recently encountered an English airman with violent tendencies. His work on the Flying Squad

meant that Greeno often interacted in an amicable manner
with the city's more crooked elements. Developing contacts and underground sources was as much a part of his
job as cracking major cases, but the street girls were dubious of Greeno's motives and kept their mouths shut. The
detective, however, did not discourage easily. Word of his
hunt spread quickly, for there were many individuals who
took a keen interest in police activity. At one point during
Greeno's inquiries, an anonymous call was placed to the
Tottenham Court Road Police Station. The caller said that
Greeno should take his search to a pub in Brixton called
the Effra Arms. Upon receiving the message Greeno—
determined to follow every possible lead that came his
way—drove his Austin to the pub on Killett Road.

The rendezvous, unfortunately, generated no viable
leads and only proved memorable in the fact that Greeno's
car was stolen while he sat inside the pub. Much to the detective's good-humored chagrin, the incident naturally
found its way into the newspapers. But powerful men in
London's criminal underworld harbored a begrudging respect for the detective and his work. When it came to light
that he owned the stolen Austin, quick action was taken to
put the deed right. As Greeno later noted: "Some smart
maneuvering was called for in the underworld to trace the
car. That didn't take long, but the thieves sent a message
back: 'We know the Guv'nor always uses his Wolseley or a
Railton. This is an Austin, so what's the game?' We convinced them that the stolen Austin was in fact a police car
used by me and it was returned within three days to the
forecourt at Scotland Yard."

Greeno continued his street-level investigation. He loitered around street corners and alleyways; he worked his
way through crowded pubs and knocked on the doors of

squalid flats. His efforts eventually paid off when he came across a woman one night in Piccadilly Circus with a story to tell. Not wanting to be seen talking to the police in public, she led Greeno to her room on Frith Street in Soho. A small, electric fire burned brightly and kept the cramped place warm. A sheet hanging from a clothesline divided the one-room flat in two. She told Greeno that on the night of Evelyn Oatley's murder she brought an airman matching Cummins's description back to her place but had not had sex with him. As the woman spoke, she noted Greeno growing increasingly distracted. He kept glancing over his shoulder and scanning the little room as if he half-expected some madman to leap out from somewhere. Indeed, as Greeno later wrote: "While I talked to her I suddenly felt we were not alone."

When he first entered the flat, he had noticed nothing unusual about the sheet, being intent as he was to hear the woman's tale. But now something about it nagged at him. The woman ignored Greeno's obvious discomfort and kept talking even when the detective stopped scribbling in his notebook. The electric fire in the far wall cast wavy shades of red and yellow on the sheet's faded surface, revealing a particular imperfection in the material: Cut in the blanket were two small holes through which a pair of bourbon-colored eyes could be seen reflecting the glow of the fire.

"While she was telling me how Cummins had brought her home, given her a couple of pounds and then leapt to his feet and vanished, I also leapt to my feet and tore down the blanket," Greeno wrote. "Behind it was a Negro."

"Please!" the woman screamed. "Don't hurt him!"

The man served as her protection, she said, and watched her when she brought clients home. He had scared the man believed to be Cummins from the apartment when the airman—taking off his clothes—caught a glimpse of the eyes behind the sheet and bolted from the premises. Had it not been for her secret guardian that night, chances are the woman would have ended up a piece of bloody wreckage like Evelyn Oatley.

DARKNESS REVEALED

FIFTEEN

The killings made the news on Valentine's Day. That Saturday morning, London residents woke to headlines declaring, "West End Search for Mad Killer." Newspaper accounts described the gruesome slaughterings and Scotland Yard's hunt for a maniac. With its flare for the dramatic, the media quickly christened the killer "The Blackout Ripper"—a moniker more suited for a comic book supervillain than a sexual deviant. But there would be little time for panic, for no sooner had the story broke, than the hunt for the Ripper had all but ended.

What made the Blackout Ripper case unique, in Greeno's estimation, was not the fact that investigators suspected a serviceman of the killings, but the rapidity with which those murders took place. In his years of service, Greeno had never seen a murderer repeatedly strike with such brutality in such a short span of time. That a serviceman was a suspect in the slayings was merely a by-product of Britain's changing wartime demographics. German bombs were not the only thing altering the British landscape. In the countryside and cities, open land was being bulldozed flat, and barracks were being built to house a newly growing segment of the population. Men in uniform were now as common on London streets as businessmen in their bowlers. But the infusion of military discipline did not mean soldiers were impervious to the lure of crime. There were barroom brawls, petty thefts, rapes, assaults and murder. The war was proving to be one of the greatest logistical challenges faced by the British legal system, for it no longer dealt solely with British subjects. Newly arrived American troops would also be brought to answer for their misdeeds in British courts.

Only three months prior, in November 1941, the barbaric acts of one military man had left the country reeling. The Yard had been called upon to investigate the savage slaying of two girls in Buckinghamshire. The bodies of eight-year-old Doreen Hearne and six-year-old Kathleen Trendle had been found in the woods, their throats having been slashed and stabbed repeatedly. The girls were last seen three days before the gruesome discovery, walking home from school. Sir Bernard Spilsbury examined the bodies at the crime scene. The girls' underclothing had been left intact, but their tops had been pulled up. Yard detectives canvassed the area and came across a khaki handkerchief bearing the laundry mark "RA 1019." Heavy rain over the previous days had made the ground soft, revealing tire tracks that came off the main road and stopped not far from where the two bodies were found.

At the point where the tire tracks stopped, a large oil patch stained the grass. Leading away from that point to where the bodies lay was a scattered trail of blood that dripped from the leaves of nearby bushes. Oil samples were collected and casts were made of the tire tracks. Detectives theorized that the killer drove his vehicle off the main road, removed the girls' bodies and carried them to where they were eventually discovered. The oil-stained ground was dug up and sent to Scotland Yard for analysis. Spilsbury took possession of the bodies and performed the postmortem.

Even for one so accustomed to the violent tendencies of man, Spilsbury was disturbed by the case. Doreen had been stabbed three times in the neck. One wound in particular highlighted the savagery of the crime. It was wider than the other two wounds, suggesting the killer had plunged his knife into the girl's throat and turned the blade repeatedly before pulling it out. A knife had been thrust into her chest six times, inflicting three puncture wounds to one of her lungs. One blow had been delivered with such force it had fractured one of her ribs. She had been partially strangled, though Spilsbury determined that the actual cause of death was hemorrhaging from the multiple stab wounds. Prior to taking her last gurgled breath, Doreen had lost six pints of blood.

Likewise, Kathleen had also died from a loss of blood. Four pints had seeped from her body. She had been stabbed eleven times in the throat, each wound measuring five-eighths of an inch wide. The power behind one blow had forced the blade of the weapon into her spinal cord. Considering the amount of blood both girls had lost, the fact that no large bloodstains had been found near the bodies confirmed what investigators already believed: The

girls had been murdered elsewhere. Yard detectives returned to Buckinghamshire, where a massive manhunt
for the killer got under way. Local residents—including
schoolchildren—were questioned and then questioned
again. Two schoolboys who spoke with police said they remembered seeing Doreen and Kathleen talking to a truck
driver on the afternoon they disappeared. Pressed for more
details, the boys told detectives the truck had been a cam-
ouflaged fifteen-hundred-weight Fordson with a canvas
top. The driver had been a young man in his mid-twenties,
who wore a service cap and steel-rimmed spectacles.

In regards to the truck, the boys said it had a Remembrance Day poppy affixed to the front radiator grill. They
said a red-and-blue square with the number 43 painted on it
in white decorated the side of a front mudguard. On the
mudguard's reverse side the boys had seen a red-colored
circle with the initials "JP" painted in blue. The number 5
was painted in blue on one of the headlamps. Detectives
recognized the described insignias as military markings and
called the War Office to find out which military regiment
they denoted. The answer turned out to be the 86th Field
Regiment of the Royal Artillery. The regiment had recently
been stationed in Buckinghamshire not far from where the
bodies were found. It had since moved to Suffolk.

Detectives feverishly pursuing the military angle quickly
discovered that the blade of a standard-issue British Army
knife measured five-eighths of an inch in width—the same
as the wounds in Kathleen's neck. Investigators continued to
question residents in the area and were able to reconstruct
the route of the military truck seen the day the girls vanished. According to witness statements, it had last been seen
along the main road that ran along the woods where the bodies were found—fourteen miles removed from the 86th

Field Regiment's old camp. Detectives traveled to the regiment's new camp in Suffolk and informed the colonel of their investigation. They told the commanding officer that the truck they were interested in had a bad oil leak. The colonel said the regiment did indeed have a truck with such a problem and took them to see the vehicle's driver, Artillery Gunner Harold Hill.

The truck was parked outside Hill's barracks, a converted barn, and appeared just as the schoolboys had described it. The Remembrance Day poppy was still affixed to the front radiator grill. Hill also matched the description the boys provided, right down to the wire-rimmed spectacles. In the back of the truck—on a sprawled-out sheet of tarpaulin—were what appeared to be bloodstains. One detective got down on all fours to peer under the truck and saw oil dripping from the rear axle. Detectives searched Hill's bunk and turned out his kit bag, finding a damp uniform in the process. When questioned as to why the clothing was wet, Hill said he had recently been caught in a sudden downpour. The telling of his story lacked conviction, and when detectives spread the uniform out on Hill's bunk, large crimson stains were clearly visible on the front, back and sleeves of the tunic. There were also dark-red spatters on the legs of the trousers.

Investigators turned up more damning evidence when shirts bearing the laundry mark "RA 1019" were dumped on the bed. An examination of the logbook in which Hill was required to track his mileage while driving the army truck further crippled his claims of innocence. His entries in the book and the actual reading on the truck's odometer were off by fourteen miles. Hill could not account for the discrepancy and bumbled his way through an unconvincing story. Because they had traveled the route from the regiment's old base to the scene where the bodies were found, detectives knew fourteen miles to be the distance between the two locations. The rope was all but placed around Hill's neck when one detective retrieved from his car the cast that had been made from the tire tracks at the crime scene. The cast matched the tire tread of Hill's truck exactly.

Hill stammered his way through one excuse after another, finally opting to play ignorant. He said he had no idea how tire tracks from his truck ended up in the woods, and asserted that he'd spent the afternoon in question reading a book in the regiment's canteen. Conveniently, he had been the only one in there at the time. And what of the handkerchief sporting his laundry mark found near the bodies? Hill—who was arrested and charged with murder—could offer no explanation for its suspicious presence.

Hill's military record revealed nothing to indicate any deviant tendencies. He was a quiet man whose stint in the army was neither exemplary nor substandard—he was simply average. He kept mainly to himself and came and went as he pleased in relative anonymity. People really didn't take much notice of him. He continued to insist he was innocent after his arrest and pleaded not guilty at his trial. Even when the Scotland Yard laboratory reported that oil taken from Hill's truck matched samples retrieved from the woods, and that the stains in the back of his truck were indeed blood and matched that of the two victims, Hill vehemently denied any wrongdoing. Ultimately, a jury thought otherwise and sentenced him to death.

But it would be an American deserter—and the young Englishwoman he seduced in a café with tales of Chicago gangsters and Hollywood glitz—who would perpetrate the most infamous wartime crime spree in Britain. Their six-day rampage culminated in the murder of a London cabbie and was immortalized in the press as "The Cleft Chin Murder," so christened after the victim's distinguishing physical characteristic. Criminal history would remember their violent rampage under the colorful names "Chicago Joe and Blondie" and the "Inky Fingers Murder." Twenty-two-year-old Karl Hulten was a private who went AWOL from his duties with the 501st Airborne Division. Eighteen-year-old Elizabeth Jones was a one-time dancer at the Blue Lagoon behind Regent Street.

After making initial acquaintance in a coffee shop near Hampstead tube station, the two embarked on a violent escapade of thievery and bodily harm in Hulten's stolen two-ton American Army truck. The shooting murder of cabbie George Heath was the climax of their adventure. Wild in the streets of London, the young couple imagined that Hulten was a Chicago gangster and that Jones was his moll. They were eventually captured driving Heath's cab. The U.S. Army permitted the British government to prosecute Hulten for murder, for which he received the death sentence. Jones—who was also convicted—was saved from the gallows by a last-minute reprieve. Although the sordid episode was quite unspectacular, the age of the criminals involved and the young couple's American mafia fantasy captivated the British public and the press. But the deadly shenanigans of Chicago Joe were far from uncommon. Numerous American and British servicemen would face tough Anglo justice. The war years would see Greeno work many crimes involving the British and American militaries. He was thrilled on one case to ride with the American Military Police, who drove around the city in powerful cars and

charged into action with guns drawn from shoulder hol-
sters. But such Hollywood-type moments would not present
themselves in the case of the Blackout Ripper—and Greeno
resigned himself to piecing together the evidence against
Gordon Frederick Cummins.

SIXTEEN

The day following Cummins's arrest, Greeno instructed Detective Sergeant Thomas Mead, "N" Division, to visit with Cummins's wife, Marjorie. They sat in the living room of the modest Cummins home. Marjorie brewed a pot of tea for herself and her visitor, but drank nothing throughout the interview. She repeatedly wiped her hands across her lap and rubbed her forehead as if attempting to ease a great ache. Since learning of her husband's arrest, she had spent the past twenty-four hours swaying on a dizzying pendulum that swung her from one depressed extreme to the next. One moment she felt mercifully numb, the next her innards were a roiling cauldron of rage and disgust. She told Mead she refused to believe her husband was capable of such brutality. She painted a picture of marital bliss. She was either unaware of—or simply could not accept—the fact that the man she married was a scoundrel. Gordon, she said, wouldn't do anything to jeopardize his chances of becoming a pilot. For this reason alone, he had refused to come home during the week in question. He wanted to make sure he was back in his billet each evening at a decent hour so that he'd be well rested for the next day's training.

"Our married life has been perfectly happy," she told Mead. "My husband has spent every available moment with me, when he was able to. I'm very surprised to hear he's been charged, as he was most anxious to do well on his training."

Mead also questioned Marjorie's sister, Freda Stevens.

"He visited her on the eighth, arriving just before lunch," she said. "He left at five. I remember at teatime I came in and saw my sister give him money. I think it was a pound. I heard Frederick say he was hard up."

"Did you notice any injuries to his left hand?" Mead asked.

Freda thought for a moment, then answered, "No."

"Cummins," wrote Greeno after the airman's arrest, "was a man of violence."

The Yard man's investigation into Gordon Frederick Cummins's nocturnal activities began at St. James's Close on February 15. He commenced his inquiries with an examination of the book all cadets were expected to sign when leaving and returning to quarters. Speaking with the on-duty sentries, Greeno learned that the men at St. James's were dismissed from duty at 5:30 p.m. and—without a late pass—were allowed to stay out until 10:30 p.m. On Saturdays, the curfew was extended to midnight. Each day saw a different orderly tasked with monitoring the book to ensure the men signed in and out as required. The record for each day was headed by the date. When signing the book, each man had to print his name, rank, service number, the Flight to which he was attached and the military time of day. The cadet charged with monitoring the book had to scribble his signature next to each entry.

Greeno stood in the billet's entry hall, studying the book. A young cadet sat nearby and gave the policeman the curious eye. It seemed apparent to Greeno that there was no strict rule as to whether the men coming and going signed the book with a pen or pencil. Although some entries were made in ink, the vast majority were scribbled across the pages in lead. Already, this meant such entries could easily be manipulated. "The booking-in book at St. James's Close is far from being a true record of absence from camp of men being off duty," Greeno wrote in his report. Several of Cummins's entries for the month of February were incomplete, for while he signed out when leaving camp, he failed to sign in several times upon his return. The entry for February 5 revealed that Cummins had left the billet at 7 p.m. According to the book, he returned to camp that night at 10 p.m.—but the checking-in time appeared to have been written with a different pencil than the other entries on the page. Noted Greeno: "It is possible that Cummins did not book in and that the book was 'written up.'"

For the night of February 7, there were no entries at all. Flipping through the book, Greeno noticed the pages for February 5 and 6 were loose, leading him to speculate that the page for February 7 had been ripped from the log. The pages were also numbered in pencil, meaning that if pages were forcibly removed, one could easily cover it up by simply renumbering them. The entries for February 8—the night of Evelyn Hamilton's murder—had simply been copied over from the page for February 6. Furthermore, there was no record in the book that Cummins had left camp the night of Evelyn Hamilton's murder—a detail Greeno hoped would not hinder the investigation. As the reliability of the book was obviously questionable, he moved on and examined the layout of the camp with a cadet as his tour guide. They went to Flat 27, where Cummins and his bunkmates were billeted in Rooms A and B. From the front, the building opened onto Prince Albert Road, while St. James's Mews ran along the back. A main hallway stretched the length of the building and provided an entrance and exit to either side of the barracks. If you were to exit the building from the back onto St. James's Mews, you would find guards to question your activities.

"Can you exit into the yard in the back without any hindrance?" Greeno asked.

"You can," answered the cadet, casting his gaze downward like a chastised child.

A stairway branching off the main hallway led up to the bunk quarters. At the top of the stairs, if you turned to the right, you would come to the entrance of Room A. A short hallway connected this room with Room B. Both rooms were similar in design, with a large window in one wall and eight bunks. Depending on where you were in one room, it was possible to stare down the short interconnecting hallway and eye the goings-on in the other room. The rooms shared a small kitchenette, from which a window led out onto a fire escape. The escape could easily be accessed without anyone in either room noticing.

"Is this used often?" Greeno asked.

The cadet shrugged. "It doubles as a fire escape and tradesman's staircase," he said. "In ordinary times, I think it would be used by tradesmen, mostly for moving goods up here rather than people."

"But it leads down to the yard in the back?" Greeno asked. "The yard along St. James's Mews?"

The cadet said it did.

"So anybody can come up from the yard, up that staircase, and enter the kitchen."

"Yes, sir," the cadet said.

Arrangements had already been made with the Royal Air Force through the Ministry of Defense to make sure Cummins's bunkmates were available for questioning at Scotland Yard's behest. Greeno and other detectives conducted the interviews over the course of several days. They tackled the week of the murders in chronological order, asking each man what he remembered about Cummins's movements. From the information he obtained, Greeno reached a blunt assessment as to Cummins's character: "He is a sexual pervert." The murder of Evelyn Hamilton proved to be the toughest case for detectives to make. There was no physical evidence tying Cummins to the crime. However, as Greeno noted in his case report, investigators were able to "link up a chain of evidence, mainly circumstantial, which it is hoped conclusively proves that the murderer is Gordon Frederick Cummins."

Even before Cummins's five bunkmates were interviewed, a discovery was made when police searched the garbage cans outside Cummins's billet on the morning of February 16. In the trash, Sergeant Alexander Findlay found a pair of rubber boot soles. A clean cut had been made across each sole near the arch prior to the sole being torn free of the boot. Each sole bore a distinctive pattern—patterns that would easily be discernible at a crime scene. It had snowed the night Evelyn Hamilton was murdered, and although no footprints were found in or around the surface shelter, Greeno believed that Cummins might have panicked at the thought of leaving such evidence behind. To cover his tracks, he removed the soles of his boots and had them replaced. There was also the matter of the injuries to Cummins's left hand, which the suspect had said were the result of working on a plane engine a few weeks back. Greeno considered it a weak excuse. Hamilton's autopsy revealed that the injuries to her neck were caused by excessive pressure applied by a left hand. It was by now known that Cummins was left-handed, for Detective Shepherd had made note of what hand the airman used to sign his statement regarding the Heywood assault. Greeno theorized that Cummins scraped his left hand against the wall or floor of the shelter when he murdered Hamilton.

"It will be remembered that the clothing of the deceased was disarranged and that inside the left leg of the bloomers and the top of the left stocking were found what appear to be small smears of blood," Greeno wrote in his report. "These, I suggest, could have been caused from blood from the injured knuckles of his left hand."

Although more coincidence than circumstantial, Greeno could not help but note the fact that both Hamilton and Cummins were knowledgeable in the field of chemistry. Police inquiries into the suspect's background revealed that Cummins was employed by the Elswick Leather Works as an assistant warehouseman in Newcastle in 1932 and lived only two blocks from Evelyn Hamilton's lodgings. Cummins's job required a minor knowledge of chemistry for the treating of the company's leather products. Nothing suggested the two were acquainted in any way, but had they indeed met the night of the murder, they would have had enough in common to converse comfortably.

"Cummins is a man who sought the company of women

at night," Greeno noted. "He is a moral pervert and frequented the Marble Arch area . . . He was billeted at [St. James's Close]—the route from there to Marble Arch, where he was in the habit of seeking the company of women, would take him in the vicinity of Gloucester Place."

Greeno believed Cummins crossed paths with Evelyn Hamilton that night while returning to his billet. He lowered her defenses with friendly conversation before lashing out. When interviewed by Greeno, Cummins's bunkmates said he was in his billet between ten and eleven on the night of the murder. "In view of this," Greeno wrote, "we must accept the fact that Cummins was in his room at the time stated by them." It was at this time, however, the detective turned his attention back to the fire escape he had seen when walking through Cummins's living quarters. "Cummins could easily have left his room when his roommates were asleep and left the billet by means of the fire escape at the rear. His roommates speak of their knowledge that the fire escape was used by residents to gain access to the building after hours unobserved. In fact, most of them admit they have used the fire escape in such circumstances."

On February 18, Greeno interviewed Air Cadet Felix Sampson, the man with whom Cummins had hit the town the night following Evelyn Hamilton's death.

"He told me he had a lot of money and wanted to spend it, and wanted someone with him as he did not want to go out on his own," Sampson told Greeno. "In fact, Cummins showed me a quantity of one-pound notes in his wallet."

This bit of information proved crucial. Had Cummins's sister-in-law, Freda Stevens, not told police that Cummins had asked his wife for some money the night of February 8, because he was "hard up"? Marjorie had only given her husband a pound, so where did this extra cash come from the following night? Although Hamilton's handbag had been found near the murder scene, her purse had not been recovered. Clare's investigation into Hamilton's background revealed that she'd earned five pounds a week as a pharmacist just prior to moving to London and often carried large sums of cash on her because of her distrust of banks.

Bolstering Greeno's theory that Cummins killed Hamilton was a discovery Clare made working his own end of the investigation. After learning an airman had been arrested for choking a woman in the West End, Clare took an immediate interest in the suspect. The similarities between the attack on Mary Heywood and the manner in which Evelyn Hamilton had died were too great to ignore. The fact that Cummins asked Heywood, according to her statement, if there were any surface air-raid shelters they could duck into resonated with Clare. On February 15, the inspector drove to the West End Police Station and examined the respirator recovered by John Shine. Removing the gas mask from its haversack, Clare discovered several pieces of mortar. He immediately sent them to the Metropolitan Police Laboratory and ordered that they be compared to the mortar scrapings taken from the surface shelter where Hamilton's body had been found. Greeno, while waiting for the laboratory to report its findings, worked Clare's discovery nicely into his theory of the crime: "It will be appreciated that some sort of a struggle must have ensued when the deceased was murdered, and if, in fact, Cummins was the murderer it is most likely that during the struggle his respirator would rub on the wall of the shelter causing mortar to fall from there and which could have fallen into the respirator haversack. It is presumed this is what happened."

The case against Cummins in the murder of Evelyn Oatley went far beyond circumstantial. Fingerprint evidence alone would likely condemn the man to the gallows. In the facts of the case, Greeno was again repulsed by Cummins's character. Evelyn Oatley's murder surpassed the brutality of Evelyn Hamilton's and also revealed Cummins's thieving nature. Although Oatley had done some business on the evening she died, police found no money in her handbag or wallet when they searched her flat. "I submit that in addition to the murderer being a person of sadistic tendencies," Greeno wrote, "he was also a thief."

Cummins concealed his violent side well from his fellow cadets. They considered him brash and cocky, but not dangerous. "Cummins seemed to be a decent sort of a fellow," Corporal John Cavendish, a roommate, told Greeno. "As far as I know, he had no particular friend among the men at Flat 27. He was not a teetotaler, but I have never seen him the worse for drink."

"Cummins always seemed cheerful and normal," another cadet told the detective, and this sentiment was echoed by others interviewed. Evidence, however, suggested something different. A left thumbprint had been found on the piece of broken mirror retrieved from Oatley's handbag, and a left little finger had left an impression on the tin opener. The Ever Ready safety razor blade and bloodied curling tongs had been found on the left side of the body at the crime scene. The tin opener had been discarded near the victim's left leg. Further damning Cummins was a discovery made the same morning Sergeant Findlay found the discarded boot soles in one of Flat 27's garbage cans. While cleaning out the cupboards in the flat's kitchenette, Sergeant Kenneth Moon found a white metal cigarette case bearing the engraved initials "L.W." Evelyn Oatley also

went by the name Leta Ward. The case was pushed back in
the far left-hand corner of the cupboard. Inside the case
was a photograph of a woman. The case was turned over to
Greeno, who showed it to Oatley's estranged husband two
days later. He identified the case as belonging to his wife
and said the picture inside was of Evelyn's mother. The last
time he had seen the case had been on February 3, while
visiting his wife in London. An explanation as to how the
case wound up in such a peculiar place was easy enough to
ascertain after Greeno interviewed Charles Johnson, the
orderly sergeant on duty at St. James's Close the night of
Cummins's arrest.

"When he returned to his billet that evening, did military police place him under arrest?" Greeno asked.

"No, sir," Johnson replied. "He walked to his living
quarters unescorted and remained there until the police
came for him several hours later."

This meant Cummins had ample opportunity to do what
he could to dispose of any evidence that might be used
against him. Greeno believed that Cummins—panicked the
police would search his bunk and discover items linking
him to the killings—had hidden Evelyn Oatley's cigarette
case in the kitchen cupboard. The fact that Cummins did
not discard the other items found on him at the time of his
arrest mystified Greeno. There were men who were forced
to kill and others who simply lost all restraint. Cummins fit
into neither category. Greeno believed the airman to be a
natural-born killer, someone who lacked the emotional
depth to feel remorse for violently depraved acts.

Throughout his investigation, Greeno attempted to be
gentle when referencing the chosen profession of the Ripper's victims. Detailing his inquiry into the murder of Margaret Lowe, the detective wrote: "The position in which the

body lay is a position which a woman of Lowe's type would assume in the course of her calling." That "position," of course, being one in which she was stretched across the bed. It became apparent to Greeno while talking to Lowe's neighbors that the woman had an unfortunate knack for soliciting the business of violent men. Tenants who lived in the same block of flats as Lowe recalled the noise of numerous late-night brawls emanating from the victim's apartment. But on the night Lowe died, there were no screams for help or din of a struggle. Indeed, her room showed no signs of disarray.

With its gruesome mutilations and various implements of death, the Lowe murder was more of a delicate matter than the previous killings, in that the victim had a child.

"I would here mention that proof of ownership by the deceased of the four knives and broken poker found on the body has not been established," Greeno wrote in his report. "They are thickly coated with blood and as the only individual who could possibly speak as to them being in the flat prior to the commission of the crime is the school-girl Barbara Lowe, who does not yet have the full circumstances of her mother's death. I have therefore refrained from showing them to her."

Cummins's bunkmates were unable to account for his whereabouts the evening Lowe was slaughtered. Fingerprints Cherrill lifted from the beer bottle in Lowe's kitchen and the candlestick holder on her mantelpiece placed a left-handed individual at the scene. "In the well of this holder were small pieces of wax—the same color as the candle which was protruding from the vagina of the body," Greeno reported after examining the evidence. "I have since tried the candle referred to in the candlestick holder, and the base of the candle fits tightly therein." The cigarette case found in Cummins's RAF tunic when he was arrested tied the airman to Lowe's apartment. Greeno sat down with Lowe's daughter on February 20, and showed her the case. The young girl immediately recognized it as her mother's.

"I've seen this case in my mother's handbag on the kitchen table and on the sideboard in the front room on many occasions," she said. "My mother was in the habit of leaving it on the kitchen table sometimes."

"And you're sure it's hers?" Greeno asked.

"It is," the girl said. "I've seen the case open in my house and remember it was a single-sided case and had a yellow band exactly like this one."

Lowe's time of death troubled Greeno, for the victim had been killed at an hour when Cummins should have been in his billet. On the street corners of Piccadilly, Greeno made the rounds armed with a photograph of Margaret Lowe. The usual response from prostitutes to questions posed by a lawman was a quick shrug of the shoulders and a terse comment about knowing nothing. In Norah Clarke, however, Greeno found a woman who had something to say. She recognized Lowe's picture and said she last saw the woman—whose pretentious manner had earned her the nickname "The Lady"—alive near the Regent Palace Hotel at 12:30 a.m. on Wednesday, February 11. Neighbors in Lowe's building told Greeno they heard Lowe return home on the night in question just after 1 a.m. Footsteps were heard leaving her apartment about an hour later.

"From the evidence available, we are forced to assume that the woman Lowe was alive at about 1:15 a.m. on Wednesday, 11th February 1942," Greeno wrote in his report. "Enquiries so far have failed, apart from fingerprints, to get Cummins near the scene of the crime at the time stated. But, as previously established, it is possible for him to leave his billet by the fire escape at night and return unnoticed in the darkness." Greeno interviewed all of Cummins's bunkmates, but none of them could recall whether they saw Cummins in bed the night of Lowe's murder. Greeno would simply have to rely on the fingerprint evidence—though it did nothing to eliminate the time discrepancy—and assume Cummins snuck in and out via the fire escape to kill.

After assembling the facts of the Lowe murder, the detective turned his attention to the events of Thursday, February 12, when the Ripper's murderous activities reached a frenzied pitch. Greeno learned through interviews with other RAF cadets that Cummins had drank that evening at the Volunteer Public House in Baker Street, arriving there at 7 p.m. and leaving approximately thirty minutes later. Accompanying Cummins on this excursion was RAF Corporal Allan Hainsworth, who was also billeted at St. James's Close. Hainsworth spoke with Greeno on February 17, and told the detective that he and Cummins had caught a taxi to the Trocadero Restaurant after leaving the Baker Street pub. On the drive over, Cummins offered to pay for the evening.

"I don't want to spend too much money tonight," Hainsworth told Cummins.

"That's all right, old boy," Cummins replied. "I have enough to see us both through."

Hainsworth told Greeno that Cummins pulled a thick roll of cash out of his tunic and slipped him a pound. He also paid the taxi driver when they reached the Trocadero. Three rounds of drinks—whiskey and beer—were purchased at the restaurant's bar and rapidly consumed before the two men sauntered over to the Universelle Brasserie a little before 7:30 p.m. Through a previous arrangement, Cummins and Hainsworth met two other cadets from St. James's Close at the Brasserie for more drinks. Cummins proved generous with his money and bought several rounds. The place had been crowded, and a blue gray fog of tobacco smoke hung heavy in the air. Men in uniform competed for female attention, and customers stood crammed shoulder to shoulder at the bar. Thus, it's not surprising that Hainsworth and the other two cadets lost sight of Cummins more than halfway through a bottle of whiskey.

"What time did this happen?" Greeno asked.

"Around 8 p.m.," Hainsworth said.

It was at this point in the evening that Cummins's attention was monopolized by Mary Heywood, who had been waiting for her army-officer friend. Reviewing Heywood's statement to the police, Greeno—like Clare—was intrigued by Cummins's inquiry as to whether there were any surface shelters in the area. It was a circumstantial tie-in to the Hamilton murder. At 10 p.m.—some fifteen minutes after Cummins attacked Heywood then fled the scene of the crime—an airman picked up prostitute Catherine Mulcahy near Oddendino's in Regent Street just off Piccadilly Circus.

The only way to tie Cummins to the Mulcahy attack was through the money he gave her. All told, Mulcahy's assailant paid her ten pounds in one-pound notes. Her prior takings that evening had been four pounds from another customer, hence it was not entirely known from whom she received which bills. Two of the pound notes, Clare noted in his report, bore consecutive serial numbers: M. 87 D 397808 and M. 87 D 397809. This prompted Greeno on February 19 to return to St. James's Close to review the billet's pay records. He spoke with Pilot Officer John Farnham Rowan, whose partial duties included acting as paying officer on the airmen's pay parades. The last payday had been Thursday, February 12.

"How is pay dispensed?" Greeno asked.

"The men are paid in alphabetical order according to their surname as listed in the pay ledger," Rowan said. "On Thursday, when I paid the men, I had a block of five hundred new one-pound Bank of England notes."

"And these notes are numbered consecutively?" Greeno asked.

"Yes," the airman said. "When I started paying out, I had the block in front of me, face upwards—that is to say, the note on top would have the lowest serial number and the one on the bottom would have the highest. But although I paid the men, I have no record of which numbers went to which man."

"Who was paid just before Cummins?"

Rowan ran his finger down a page in the pay ledger. "That would be Corporal Critchley, Corporal Crook and Air Cadet Crozier."

"Are any of them here today?"

Corporal Robert Ramsay Critchley was sitting on his bunk idly flipping through a newspaper when Greeno approached him and identified himself.

"You were paid last Thursday, Corporal?"

"Yes, sir," Critchley said.

"How much?"

"I was paid four pounds in new one-pound Bank of England notes," Critchley said.

"I don't suppose you still have them."

"As a matter of fact, I do," the airman said, reaching for a satchel at the end of his bunk. He fished around inside it and retrieved three of the notes. "I did spend one of them yesterday to buy a registered envelope from the post office at the top of St. John's Wood High Street."

He handed the notes to Greeno, who immediately made note of the serial numbers: M. 87 D 397799, 397800 and 397801. "So the bill you spent must have had the serial number 397798 or 397802?"

"Yes, sir," Critchley said. "I suppose so."

Greeno returned to Rowan with the serial numbers from Critchley's notes and asked how much the two men standing in line between Critchley and Cummins were paid.

Consulting his ledger, Rowan told Greeno that Corporal Crook was paid four pounds in one-pound notes, and Air Cadet Crozier was paid two pounds in one-pound notes. Greeno did the math. If the bill Critchley spent was numbered 397798, that would mean Crook was paid with notes numbering 397802 through 397805. Crozier would have been paid next, with notes 39806 and 39807.

"After Crozier, how much was Cummins paid?" Greeno asked.

"Two pounds," Rowan said, consulting the ledger.

This would mean Cummins had been paid with notes bearing the serial numbers 39808 and 39809. "Thus it is conclusively proved that Cummins was paid the two one-pound notes, which were amongst the ten one-pound notes he gave to the woman Catherine Mulcahy," Greeno wrote in his report. Doris Jouannet—at this point in the evening—had still been alive. Canvassing the streets with a picture of Jouannet in hand, Greeno learned from several surprisingly talkative prostitutes that the woman had been seen soliciting clients near Edgware Road at about 10:30 p.m. Mulcahy had told investigators her assailant fled her flat at 11 p.m. Something in particular struck Greeno about Mulcahy's statement: "It is of importance to note that it is a usual thing for men, when they go home with her to her flat, especially from Piccadilly, to ask how they get back. Mulcahy invariably replies, 'Go out, turn right then left and straight up to Edgware Road,' but she does not remember whether she told this to the airman. This direction would of course take the individual who left her flat into Sussex Gardens at a time when the deceased—Doris Jouannet—was thereabouts soliciting prostitution and I submit brings Cummins at the right hour to the vicinity of the scene of this crime."

Although Greeno's theory was circumstantial in basis, plenty of physical evidence tied Cummins to Jouannet's murder—specifically, the comb with broken teeth he had been carrying when arrested and the engraved fountain pen found in his kit bag. On February 14, the day following Cummins's apprehension, Henry Jouannet was shown the pen and the comb. He identified both items as belonging to his dead wife.

"I remember the day my wife bought the comb," he told detectives. "It was at a street market, and we got into an argument because it had teeth missing. I told her I'd buy her a proper one, but she insisted on getting that one."

There had also been the watch—identified by Henry Jouannet as belonging to his wife—found in the carrying case to Cummins's gas mask. The watch's worn-out strap had been secured with strips of Elastoplast—the same kind found in Doris Jouannet's bedroom. Police-lab comparisons confirmed that the strips of tape wrapped around the watch came from the roll of Elastoplast found in the bedroom.

"We are able to prove," Greeno wrote in summarizing the case as a whole, "that Cummins was a man of violence and that he associated with prostitutes."

On March 19, 1942, Greeno submitted his report to the superintendent of Scotland Yard.

SEVENTEEN

Detective Chief Inspector Edward Greeno—in the company of Divisional Detective Inspector Leonard Clare and Sergeant Alexander Findlay—drove to Brixton Prison on the afternoon of February 16, to interview the suspected killer. What they saw in the interview room surprised them. Two days in custody had done nothing to dull Cummins's natural polish. His ramrod-straight posture as he sat in his chair—and his amicable smile—leant him an air of unruffled sophistication. When he spoke, he did so in a calm and friendly manner, never raising his voice or conveying anger through expression. Prison officials had supplied Greeno with the clothing Cummins was wearing and the possessions he'd had on him at the time of his arrest and booking. Cummins quietly watched Greeno as the detective flipped through the booking report. Greeno read the details relating to Cummins's clothing: "Seven small red stains were on the left side of the chest below the arm.

Three small well-defined stains were on the upper part of the right side of the chest and there was one small red stain one and a half inches above the lower hem on the front to the right of the mid-line."

According to the report, the stains were not blood. They were the result of a nitrocellulose dope containing iron oxide. One bloodstain, however, had been found on the shirt just above the first buttonhole. Blood had also been found on the belt of Cummins's uniform. Two stains—each measuring about an inch in length—were clearly visible on the belt's inner surface. One was in the front near the buckle; the other was in the back. Greeno handed the report to Clare and pulled out a notepad. Cummins remained silent; that smile of his never wavering.

"My name is Detective Chief Inspector Edward Greeno," the detective said. "I am conducting investigations relative to the murder of three women during last week: one case at 153 Wardour Street, W.1.; another at Flat 4, 9/10 Gosfield Street, W.1., near Great Portland Street in the Tottenham Court Road area; and another in a flat at No. 187 Sussex Gardens, Paddington, near Edgware Road. I should like you, if you will, to tell me your movements on and from Sunday, the eighth of February 1942, and the following days of the week."

"Yes," said Cummins, almost sounding bored and nodding like a man in casual conversation. "Certainly."

He leaned forward, folding his hands in front of him, and began talking. He said he had spent all of Sunday, February 8, in the company of his wife and sister-in-law. They parted ways at eight that evening. He stopped off at a local pub for a whiskey before catching the No. 9 bus to Hammersmith. From there, he caught a train to Baker Street and had been back in his billet just shy of 10 p.m. He promptly

went to bed and remained there until six-thirty the following morning. Monday, February 9, had been spent working
in the recruitment center at St. James's Close, Cummins
said. He left camp at 6 p.m. in the company of Air Cadet
Sampson. Cummins told police he and Sampson dined at
Martinez's in Swallow Street before embarking on the evening's carnal adventure.

"At Piccadilly Circus we saw two prostitutes, and we
spoke to them," Cummins said. "My friend went off with the
dark one and I went off with the fair one, arranging to meet
my friend at the same spot. No definite time was made for the
meeting on return, as the girls said, 'We'll bring you back.'"

Cummins said he and the girl had agreed on a price of
one pound.

"I gave her a pound note when I got to her room, where
there was a fire in the grate," he said. "The woman, I am almost certain, took all her clothes off. I removed my respirator, greatcoat and cap and put them down somewhere in
the room and sat in the armchair and undid the flies on my
trousers. I was quite happy lying back in the chair with this
woman standing naked in front of me. The woman had a
reasonable figure but was a bit on the thin side. She started
playing with my person, but because I had drunk so much,
I couldn't do anything."

Thwarted by drink, Cummins got out of the chair, put
his clothes back on and left to meet his friend, he said. The
woman accompanied him back to Piccadilly Circus, where
the other prostitute stood waiting.

"Your friend was here a minute ago," she told Cummins. "If you shout, you'll probably catch him."

Cummins told Greeno that he left the women and began
walking toward Regent Street, shouting his friend's name.
They met in Piccadilly Circus at about 10 p.m.

"He answered when I was somewhere near Oddendino's near the arches," he said. "We met and spoke about there not being too much time to waste, so we crossed over Regent Street and caught a bus to Marble Arch."

Cummins said his recollections of that evening were blurred by the bottle, but he vaguely recalled that he and Sampson—at some point—took a bus to St. John's Church. They walked from there back to their billets.

"The next morning our roommates remarked on how drunk we were and on the fact they had to help put us to bed," Cummins said.

Greeno interrupted him. "What are the names of these roommates?"

"Flight Sergeant Snelus, DFM, Corporal Cavendish and Sergeant Moon."

"And what about Tuesday, February 10?" Greeno asked.

Cummins said he was inoculated that afternoon and, because the shot left his right arm feeling sore, opted for a quiet night in. This was just as well, he said, for the previous night's bender had reduced him to thrusting his face in the toilet bowl throughout the course of the day. He sipped scalding black tea that evening at the YMCA Forces House and listened to one of his fellow cadets play the piano. He called his wife at 8 p.m. and was in bed with the lights out less than two hours later.

"When I went to my room, I don't remember seeing anyone to speak to," Cummins said. "I slept right through to Wednesday morning. I got up shortly after reveille and did not leave camp all day. As I was still feeling the ill effects of the inoculation, I did not go out that night either. From seven to eight that evening I was at the YMCA and then came back to my billet. When I came to bed, there was no one in the room, but all the other members of my room must have seen me there when they came in later."

Cummins said he spent Thursday engaged in various military activities. There was marching and parading, and other routines he found worthless in their overall contribution to the war effort. It had also been payday.

"The morning was filled by pay parade," Cummins said. "I got paid about half past ten to eleven and received two one-pound notes and a 10/- note. This is a fortnight's pay—we are paid fortnightly."

That evening, he said, he went with another airman to the Universelle Brasserie. Alcohol was consumed in liberal quantities, for neither Cummins nor his friend saw the point of moderation. More than several rounds were successfully downed before their surroundings took on a somewhat tremulous quality. Deciding he was through, Cummins staggered away from the bar, only to reconsider retiring for the night when he spotted Mary Heywood sitting by herself.

"Tell me what happened," Greeno said.

"At the beer bar my friend began speaking to some male acquaintance, and I went to the spirit bar, where I had some brandy and whiskey," Cummins said. "I then remember speaking to a woman."

Greeno suddenly stopped him.

"You don't have to make a statement as to what you said to the woman," Greeno said. "Anything you say will be taken down in writing and may be submitted as evidence."

"I want to give an account of all my movements," Cummins said. "The woman was sitting at the foot of the stairs and obviously looking for a man. We had a few words and I think I brought her a drink, then we left the spirit bar together."

Cummins told Greeno he may have taken the woman to another pub for a drink, but couldn't be sure. He repeated what he had told Shepherd three days prior at the West End Central Police Station, that he dimly remembered walking around the streets with her, listening to the incorporeal sounds of the city. The specifics of what might or might not have happened next were obscured by a whiskey-colored fog.

"I don't remember anything else about her," he said. "The next thing I recall is standing in Piccadilly Circus and talking to another woman. She said, 'Would you like to come home with me?' She said she was twenty-two and had two children."

She was dressed in all black, Cummins said.

"I should describe her as very good-looking," he said. "She had gray eyes—widely spaced—and auburn hair that fell to the nape of her neck. I liked her in her black-tailored coat and skirt. She was tall and thin with a very good fig-ure. I agreed to go home with her, and we took a taxi from Regent Street. She gave the driver her address, and the driver of the cab put us down in a side street off Edgware Road near Marble Arch. I paid him, but I cannot remember how much I gave him."

Cummins said he was unfamiliar with the location and asked the woman what the easiest route back to St. Johns's Wood would be.

She pointed toward Marble Arch and explained, "You turn right from the arch and take the first left, which will bring you to Edgware Road. Would you like to come in now?"

Cummins said he would.

"We went to her flat, which was in the mews under the arch about halfway down on the right-hand side and above a motor hire company," Cummins said. "She took me upstairs to the floor above the garage—it was the only floor in the building—and we sat chatting for some time. Eventually, I gave her a pound and we both got on the bed."

The woman stripped for Cummins and removed his trousers and shirt. She climbed on top off him, her mildly shampoo-scented hair hanging down the sides of her face as she rolled a condom on him. He breathed in her perfume and raised his mouth to meet hers.

"We had intercourse," Cummins said. "It was then very late. I thought it was between one and two o'clock in the morning and I told her I had to leave. So I left, and left her on the landing in her pajamas, and let myself out."

Cummins said he followed the woman's directions and eventually found himself on Oxford Street. He caught a taxi and returned to his billet.

"I asked the driver for the time. He said he did not know, but remarked, 'It's getting on a bit,'" Cummins said. "I then went to my billet, where I was detained by the guard commander until the arrival of the police. The two women, whom I mentioned as going to their flats with, are the only two women of that nature I have been with for about two years. I have not been in any other flats in London with any women."

Greeno said nothing. Instead, he spread a morbid collage of photographs out on the table. Margaret Lowe was presented to Cummins in grisly black-and-white, her abdomen slashed and the bloodied knives used in the killing placed carefully on her exposed thigh. With a ligature tied around her neck and frothy blood dripping from her nose and mouth, Doris Jouannet was placed beside Margaret. Rounding out this grim trio was Evelyn Oatley lying on a bloodstained sheet with a crimson-smeared flashlight protruding from her vagina. Greeno straightened the images and sat silently for a moment, allowing Cummins to examine the carnage.

The airman, completely unmoved, briefly studied the images. He gave Greeno an almost quizzical stare as if wondering what the detective expected from him.

"You have never been to a flat near Tottenham Court Road or in the vicinity thereof with any woman?" Greeno asked. "What about Gosfield and Wardour streets, or Sussex Gardens?"

Cummins's tone of voice remained amicable.

"I have never been to a flat near Tottenham Court Road," he said. "And I don't know Gosfield Street—had I been there, I would have remembered it. I have never been with a woman in any flat in Sussex Gardens, though I know where these are. I know Wardour Street, and the flat to which I took the fair girl on Monday night may have been on Wardour Street. But again, I have never been in any other flat in this area with any other women."

Greeno placed the fountain pen with the initials "D.J." etched into its gold band on top of the photographs. Next to it, he put the wristwatch with the Elastoplast strips wrapped around the band.

"That pen is not mine," Cummins said without prompting. "I have never seen it before."

"And the watch?" Greeno asked.

"That watch is not mine," Cummins said. "I saw it for the first time at the West End Central Police Station, when it was taken from a service respirator case I was carrying when arrested, but which was not mine. I don't know whose respirator it is. I picked it up at the Brasserie on Thursday night at about nine or nine-thirty just before I left the spirit bar."

Cummins's attempt to explain away the watch as an unfortunate twist of fate left Greeno unmoved. In response, the detective cast a quick glance under the table and asked the airman if he was still wearing his RAF-issued boots. Cummins said he was.

"Can you take them off, please?" Greeno asked.

Cummins did as instructed and slid the boots across the floor to the detectives. Findlay picked them up and examined the soles.

"Brand-new," he said. He reached into a bag and retrieved the soles recovered from the trash at St. James's. They fit perfectly over the bottom of Cummins's boots. When Findlay asked the airman what compelled him to replace a perfectly good pair of soles, Cummins simply offered a nonchalant shrug. Findlay bagged the boots as evidence and slid Cummins a pair of prison-issued shoes. Cummins tried on the new footwear and voiced his approval.

Greeno cleared the table and put the pictures, watch and pen away. "As a result of inquiries I have made," he said, "you will be brought up at Bow Street Police Court tomorrow morning and charged with murder."

Cummins raised an eyebrow. "How many women did you say?"

"Three," Greeno said.

"And I'm to be charged in their deaths?"

"Yes."

The airman nodded, but said nothing. "At the time of the interview," Greeno later noted, "he was quite rational."

Rational he might have been, but Cummins—throughout his statement—had been vague with times. Too much drinking, he said, had dulled the focus of his recollections, but the events of the evenings—as he relayed them—were correct, as far as he was concerned. It was just possible that Cummins believed his own lies. Greeno had seen such men delude themselves before, but Cummins's demeanor was particularly sinister. His manner of banter suggested some-one in a jovial frame of mind, not the least bit concerned with the pressing circumstance in which he found himself. Most men, if presented with irrefutable evidence of their crime—as Greeno had done with Cummins—would at least show a weakening in their facade. The airman had revealed nothing, his face betraying no sense of inner turmoil. In fact, he seemed incapable of emotion. To Greeno, the air-man came across as incredibly vain—as the sort of man who takes great pleasure in admiring himself. Perhaps Cummins had rehearsed for an occasion such as this, studying the layout of his face each morning in the mirror. Who knows how long he had practiced concealing his real character from others. The young man knew how to work his face, manipulate its handsome features to convey a look of perpetual innocence when need be. But what had given rise to Cummins's violent impulses, and how many times had he exercised them in the past?

EIGHTEEN

On the morning of February 17, one day before his twenty-eighth birthday, Gordon Frederick Cummins appeared at the Bow Street Police Court—the very place where Sir Henry Fielding had set in motion the evolution of Scotland Yard nearly two hundred years prior—and was charged with the murders of Evelyn Oatley, Margaret Lowe and Doris Jouannet. Evidence was lacking to bring charges in the murder of Evelyn Hamilton. Cherrill fingerprinted the airman following the arraignment and asked him to sign the fingerprint card. Cummins took Cherrill's pen in his left hand and scribbled his name on the signature line. The formalities of arraignment completed, Cummins was led out the back entrance, bundled into a police car and returned to Brixton Prison to await his trial, scheduled to start in April.

Although Greeno and other investigators were confident they had their man, they were puzzled as to his motives.

While the crimes were sexual in nature, Cummins's past revealed nothing that would hint at violent sexual proclivities. As Greeno wrote in his report shortly after Cummins's apprehension: "On forms filled in and signed by him when applying for service in the Royal Air Force, a declaration is made by Cummins that he has never suffered from any mental trouble or serious disease, and has never been injured."

But anyone could lie about such things.

Cummins had lied to Greeno during their prison interview. For some, lying is a subtle art entailing careful consideration for the fact one wishes to distort. The trick is to delicately insert your fabrication into a mostly true narrative, rendering it false in a manner that is not easily detectable. Cummins's lies, however, were so obvious that there was little challenge in disproving them. The matter of Cummins's alibi for the night of Evelyn Oatley's murder was a prime example. Greeno dealt with it easily by firing a few well-placed questions at Air Cadet Felix Sampson, who had ventured out with Cummins that night. Greeno spoke with Sampson two days after interviewing Cummins, who said he and Sampson had returned to their barracks together after a night of heavy drinking. Sampson, however, told Greeno that no such thing occurred. After securing the services of two prostitutes, he and Cummins lost touch for the remainder of the evening, Sampson said, telling Greeno he snuck into the barracks shortly before sunrise and found Cummins already in bed. Cummins told Sampson he had sought a frolic with another woman because the first did not meet his sexual standards.

"Did he tell you what time he got back to the billet?" Greeno asked.

"He said it was about three-thirty," Sampson said.

If true, the information placed Cummins in the West

End at the time of Evelyn Oatley's murder. And what reason did Sampson have to lie? He freely admitted that his desire for more bedroom high jinx that night resulted in him missing curfew. If he'd wanted to spare himself the trouble of an RAF reprimand, Sampson could have concealed that truth and covered for Cummins at the same time. The statements of other cadets confirmed Sampson's version of events. None of the men questioned said they ever recalled an evening where Sampson and Cummins returned to the barracks too drunk to get into bed unassisted. This also directly contradicted what Cummins had told Greeno. Why would he tell such blatant lies that were so easily blown apart? Greeno did not believe Cummins to be stupid. Instead, perhaps, an overpowering ego—a sense of intellectual superiority—consumed the airman. Maybe ingrained in Cummins's psyche was the overwhelming belief that the police would blunder the case. His arrest had not been the result of clever investigative work, but merely a misstep on his part. Had he remembered his gas mask when fleeing the approaching John Shine, Scotland Yard detectives would still be wandering around in a haze of ignorance. They were dumb animals. Or maybe the reasoning behind Cummins's blatant untruths was far less clinical. Maybe he had lied so often to himself that he believed the fallacies to be fact. Greeno remained unsure which one of his theories—if either—accounted for the airman's stubborn detachment from reality. Most killers Greeno had interviewed over the years revealed some reasoning behind their actions in the answers to simple questions. Cummins, however, had shed light on nothing. It served to only deepen the mystery of his persona.

Police interviewed members of Cummins's family, all of whom were shocked by the allegations. His marriage seemed harmonious, and his childhood seemed to have been completely normal. He was born on February 18, 1914, at New Easwick, York. Educated at Llandovery County Intermediate Secondary School and the Northampton Town and County Secondary School for Boys, he obtained a diploma in chemistry at the age of sixteen. Despite this accomplishment, his classroom performance could only be described as poor. Socializing seemed to take greater precedent than schoolwork. He nevertheless applied—and was accepted—to the Northampton College of Technology as a full-time leather student, and brought his miserable study habits with him. College records were blunt in their assessment of Cummins as being lazy and completely lacking in motivation.

Tired of the constant hounding from his professors, he left the college on November 1, 1932, and sought to establish a career on his own terms. He moved to Newcastle and landed a job with the Elswick Leather Works as an assistant warehouseman. He survived in this capacity until April the following year, when his boss let him go because of his poor on-the-job performance. Like the young schoolboy he used to be, the older Cummins had been hard-pressed to apply himself to the necessary tasks at hand. His workplace superiors—much like his teachers before them—found him shiftless. He bounced from job to job until August 1933, when he took employment at the factory of George Barker and Limited in his old stomping grounds of Northampton. Here he got a job as a leather tanner—a trade that made direct use of his studies in chemistry and leatherwork. Although he had pursued such subjects in school, the quality of his work suggested that he had failed to retain much of what he had learned. The factory foreman continued giving Cummins chances in the hopes the young man would improve, but such improvement never came. In September

1934, Cummins again found himself unemployed. "Cummins," said his boss "is rather dense."

Cummins decided to try his hand at bigger things and moved to London the following month. He found work at Reptile Dressers Limited as a leather dresser and began training to be a foreman in the company's factory. He brought home three pounds a week. Not wanting to squander his money on food and heat, Cummins etched out a fast-paced existence for himself. He enjoyed the pleasures of drinking and the company of women. As he eventually would his fellow cadets in the Royal Air Force, Cummins regaled his factory coworkers with explicit tales of sexual conquest. Arriving at work some mornings, his rough appearance—ruffled hair, bloodshot eyes and the first slight hint of a beard—spoke of a wild previous evening. The job was nothing more than a way to support his raunchy pursuits, of which there were many in London. The young man, by this point, had affected his pretentious accent and the stories of his noble lineage. The effect this facade of personality had on the opposite sex was staggering, and he used it to the best of his ability. Too much drinking and sex, however, had a negative impact on his job performance. It soon became apparent to Cummins's superiors at Reptile Dressers that easy women and cheap drinks were of more interest to him than showing up for work on time. On February 8, 1935, Cummins was fired. Company records described him as "irresponsible . . . and fond of the company of women."

Out of work and out of cash, Cummins moved in with his brother, John Harry Cummins, at Mews Flat, Queens Mews, Bayswater. He lounged about the city, working the occasional odd job to line his pockets. His enthusiasm for women and drink never abated, but his family soon made it clear that they expected more from him. In a somewhat surprising move, he joined the Royal Air Force as a flight rigger on November 11, 1935—a bold step for one with no sense of discipline or respect for authority. His brother, John, would go on to become a sublieutenant in the Royal Navy Volunteer Reserve.

Although Cummins would carry his womanizing ways with him into the military, nothing suggested he had the makings of a violent sexual predator. Once apprehended, he still offered no clues as to what propelled him to commit such heinous deeds. In the wake of his initial interview with Cummins at Brixton Prison, Greeno made note of the airman's apparent normality: "He is a well-spoken individual and of good appearance, and when interviewed by me was quite normal and was possessed of his full faculties. Knowledge so far as to his antecedent history, discloses in him no mental derangement."

Perhaps the force that drove Cummins to kill would be revealed at trial.

Following Cummins's formal arraignment at Bow Street, Cherrill hastily returned to the Yard and compared the airman's prints with those lifted from the crime scenes. The fact that Cummins was left-handed already told Cherrill what the print analysis would reveal. Cherrill retrieved from the case file in his office the latent prints he had been able to lift from items found in the victims' flats. The first set of prints to be compared with Cummins's were those lifted from the bottle of stout, the drinking glass and the candlestick taken from Margaret Lowe's apartment. Inspector Percy Law of the Photographic Section made enlargements of the impressions for easier examination. Cherrill brought them back to his office and began the meticulous process of mapping each print, numerically marking their varying characteristics—characteristics he expected to see in Cummins's prints. It always proved to be tedious work. One had to account for distortions in the crime-scene impressions. The surface of the objects from which they were lifted could slightly bend or alter the prints, but the ridge characteristics would remain unchanged.

There were numerous characteristics Cherrill was looking for, from the stopping and starting points of various ridges to their individual branch patterns. Such details are evident only to the properly trained eye. There's bifurcation, when a single ridge breaks off into two ridges. A bifurcation can form a spur, which is the result of a short ridge branching off a longer one. A ridge might bifurcate then reunite as a single ridge, while another might run between two parallel ridges. There are also independent ridges equal in length and width, known as dots. Once these characteristics are pinpointed on one crime-scene print, an examination of the suspect's prints can begin. Points of similarity are found when the characteristics of the crime-scene print are located in the same position and relation to other ridges on the suspect's prints. For example, if a spur is separated from a dot by three ridges in the same location on each print, a point of similarity has been found. Despite the intricacies of the search, it did not take long before Cherrill found points of similarity between the prints on the candlestick and Cummins's right ring finger. In total, sixteen such points were identified.

Another print on the candlestick was made by the little finger on Cummins's right hand. Again, sixteen points of similarity were pinpointed. A print on the beer glass shared sixteen points of similarity with the airman's right middle finger. The beer bottle had prints from Cummins's right thumb, right forefinger and right little finger. In each instance, Cherrill found sixteen points of similarity. Items removed from the other crime scenes proved just as damning. More than a dozen matching characteristics were found on the little finger of Cummins's left hand and a print lifted from the tin opener used to mutilate Evelyn Oatley. The thumbprint found on a piece of broken mirror in Evelyn's apartment shared more than two dozen points of similarity with Cummins's left thumb.

No usable prints were found at the Jouannet crime scene. Likewise, the surface shelter where Evelyn Hamilton had been found yielded no discernible impressions. The shelter, however, did surrender one secret in the mortar scrapings that Clare ordered be collected as evidence. In early March, the Metropolitan Police Laboratory completed its comparison of the scrapings from the shelter and the mortar sample found in Cummins's gas mask. According to the lab's report: "The mortar from the gas mask and those samples taken from the outside wall of shelter and inside wall of shelter were of similar appearance and had the same characteristics. Analysis showed that the mortar from the gas mask had a slightly closer resemblance to the mortar taken from the inside of the shelter than to that from the outside. The material from the floor consists of a mixture of powdered mortar similar to the other samples and ordinary dirt." Subsequently, the airman was charged in the murder of Evelyn Hamilton.

Cummins was a model prisoner during his time at Brixton. He made no fuss and caused no trouble with the guards. Not once did he lose his pompous air, express remorse for his actions or voice regret over his current predicament. The prison's senior medical officer, Hugh Grierson, MB, kept Cummins under continuous observation. In a report dated April 13, 1942, Grierson recorded his thoughts on the prisoner: "Throughout the period he has been under my care here, the accused has been normal in conduct and rational in conversation. At no time has he exhibited any evidence of mental disease. Though apparently the unemotional type, he has not exhibited a lack of interest at interviews. He denies any loss of memory or blackouts at any time in his life. He states he was a moderate drinker until he joined the Royal Air Force in 1935, but since this has drunk more heavily."

During one interview, Grierson brought up the violent nature of the crimes with which Cummins had been charged.

"The character and sites of the wounds inflicted on the victims points to a sadistic basis for the murders," Grierson told the airman.

Cummins simply shook his head and denied "any perversion or deviation from the normal."

"According to Cummins's father," Grierson noted, "there is no history of insanity in the family nor has his son ever shown any evidence of mental disorder. He adds that his son has always been a normal person and 'without any cruelty in his nature.'"

NINETEEN

On Thursday, April 23, 1942, Gordon Frederick Cummins appeared at the Old Bailey in front of Mr. Justice Asquith to enter his plea on four counts of murder and two counts of attempted murder. On each charge, Cummins—neatly turned out in a dark suit—pleaded not guilty. Immediately thereafter, his trial got under way. Prosecuting the case were Christmas Humphreys and G. B. McClure of the Crown Prosecution Service. Appearing on behalf of the defense were John Flowers and Victor Durand. It was a solemn affair replete with the dark robes and powdered wigs of a British legal proceeding.

The jury of twelve men, having duly been sworn, was addressed by the clerk: "Members of the jury, the prisoner at the bar, Gordon Frederick Cummins, is charged upon indictment with the murder of Evelyn Oatley on the tenth day of February of this year. To this indictment he has pleaded that he is not guilty. It is your charge to say, having heard the evidence, whether he be guilty or not."

Although he was charged with multiple counts of murder, the prosecution tried Cummins on a solitary charge—such is the norm in British courts when a person stands trial for multiple crimes. It was, Cherrill noted in his memoirs, "an example of the scrupulous fairness with which justice is administered in our courts." Although Oatley had been the second of Cummins's four murder victims, she was the first with which police were able to confirm Cummins's role in the death through fingerprints. The defendant stood at the bar throughout the proceedings and maintained his outward appearance of calm. He casually joked with his lawyers and often chuckled to himself. Occasionally, he turned to smile and wave at his wife, who sat in the public gallery. Even now, Marjorie could not accept that her husband was a man of exceptional cruelty and violence.

Cummins's trial was largely unspectacular, save for a judicial misstep that derailed the proceedings. The mishap occurred while Frederick Cherrill was on the stand, explaining the points of similarity between prints lifted from items recovered at the victim's apartment and those taken from Cummins following his arraignment. Photographic enlargements of the crime-scene prints were handed to the jurors for closer inspection. As jurors passed the images among themselves, Cherrill—from the witness stand—noticed something amiss. The jurors had inadvertently been handed pictures from another Ripper murder, not that of Evelyn Oatley. Even from the witness stand, Cherrill—familiar as he was with the nature of the evidence—could see the discrepancy. He turned to the judge and whispered, "I think the jury has been handed the wrong exhibit."

It became immediately obvious to the jurors that something was not right, for the images they were examining did not match those that had been placed on an easel for the rest of the courtroom to see. Their quizzical looks caught the attention of the judge and the lawyers. The pictures were promptly removed from the jury's possession, but it was too late—the trial had been compromised. The jury was excused while attorneys for both sides addressed the issue with Justice Asquith. Following a lengthy discussion on the mishap's possible ramifications, Asquith recalled the jury, only to immediately dismiss them.

"It is possible, and very probable," the judge told the jurors, "that from the exhibit before you, you might have drawn certain inferences which would have made it impossible for you to try this action properly."

"It was the first time in the history of the Old Bailey that a trial had ever been stopped for such a reason," Cherrill wrote in his memoirs. Court reconvened on Monday, April 27, with a new jury of twelve men. The prosecution's opening statement to the newly seated panel was forceful and to the point, yet delivered with all the politeness one would expect in an English court.

"May it please Your Lordship," Humphreys said, addressing the courtroom. "Gentlemen of the jury, I am instructed to prosecute in this case, with my friend Mr. McClure, and the prisoner, who is a cadet in the Royal Air Force, and is defended by my friends Mr. Flowers and Mr. Durand. The charge is that of the murder of a Mrs. Oatley, who was known to her friends as Leta Ward."

Humphreys told the jury that the victim, "in the absence of her husband, practiced on the streets of London, at times, as a prostitute." He summarized the finding of Oatley's body by the meter readers and detailed the savage nature of the injuries suffered in her final moments. "She had, so the medical evidence will say, and I think there will be no dispute about it, been strangled, in the sense that someone had gone a long way towards strangling her with his hands on her neck, sufficiently far to render her unconscious."

He paused and looked hard at Cummins. "Then," he continued, "she had her throat cut—a deep cut right across the side of the neck, causing tremendous loss of blood and, shortly after, death. And, just before she died, and when she was unconscious, the person who had done this had also inflicted a series of jagged stab wounds in the pubic hair and round the entrance to the vagina."

As jury members shifted uncomfortably in the their seats, Humphreys told them of the large pool of blood that had formed on the floor as it spilled from the jagged wound in the victim's neck. He made reference to the bloody tin opener and safety razor blade found at the scene. "These weapons were used by this person, whoever he was, to murder Mrs. Oatley, and the prosecution will ask you to say that you are satisfied," Humphreys said, then pointed to Cummins. "And the prosecution will further ask you to say that you are satisfied, upon the evidence they will call before you, that this man was the murderer, and no other."

The evidence he outlined—focusing heavily on fingerprints—was damning.

"You will hear evidence from one of the greatest experts in the country upon fingerprints," Humphreys said. "He will tell you that there have been some half-million fingerprints taken in his time and there have never been two alike."

Cummins stood at the bar and smiled as Humphreys explained to jurors how easy it was for cadets at St. James's Close to sneak in and out of their billet via the fire escape, and how the defendant's statement to the police as to his activities on the night of February 9 differed from that of his friend, Felix Sampson. Then, of course, there was the fact that Evelyn Oatley's cigarette case had been found in the kitchen of Cummins's billet.

"The prosecution would ask you to say, each one of you, that you are satisfied, on the evidence which will be called before you, and upon nothing else," Humphreys said in conclusion, "that this man is the man who murdered Mrs. Oatley on the tenth of February."

The case against Cummins seemed without flaw and left the defense few options. Cummins's attorneys attacked Scotland Yard's methods, attempting to portray its investigators as being loose with the facts and vindictive toward the accused. On the stand, Frederick Cherrill found the quality of his fingerprint work called into question.

"I suppose it is difficult for anybody, in a way, to challenge your specific knowledge of this branch of science, is it not?" Flowers asked. "Have other people quite the same knowledge of fingerprints as you, or are you sort of alone in the country on this?"

"Oh, no," Cherrill said.

"It is limited, I suppose, to the police force?"

"I think there are a few amateurs about."

"I suppose," Flowers said, "you would not put the opinion of an amateur as being anywhere near as worthy of credence as yours?"

"Hardly, sir."

"I must challenge you a little with regard to this matter," Flowers said, turning his attention to the fingerprint lifted from the handle of the tin opener. "It's a very imperfect mark."

"Well, not for a mark that has been put on metal," Cherrill

said. "If you put a mark upon there again, you would have the same effect."

"It's very faint," Flowers said. "Would you, with regard to that mark, stake your reputation, knowing that a man is being tried for his life?"

Cherrill was unhesitant: "Yes."

Concerning Flowers was the difference in the distance between certain points of similarity on the print lifted from the tin opener and the corresponding fingerprint taken from the defendant on the day of his arraignment. Both the print lifted from the opener and the print taken from Cummins had been enlarged six times their original size and placed side by side on an easel in front of the jury box.

Looking at the images, Flowers said, "I gather the reason for the difference in distance between certain marks may be explained by the fact that the mark is on the curved area of the tin opener, whereas his print is taken from a flat surface."

"Only partly," Cherrill said. "The finger is not a cast-iron object. It is plastic. You can move it about. You can move flesh."

"That I understand, but you are not suggesting that if I press my thumb upon that piece of wood hard," Flowers said, motioning to the judge's bench, "and then I put it upon there not so hard, the difference in distance will not be infinitesimal, are you?"

"They would be very great in an enlarged photograph," Cherrill said. "I have known a fingerprint to extend four millimeters with different pressure."

"Perhaps it is a matter of common sense," Flowers said. "I want really to ask you questions about the thumb mark on the mirror, which was a flat surface. That is, of course, a much clearer mark than the tin opener."

On the easel in front of the jury, Flowers placed an enlarged image of the print lifted from the piece of broken mirror found in Evelyn Oatley's handbag. Next to it, he placed the enlarged image of Cummins's left thumbprint.

"You have pointed out on the photographs, by your marks, certain points of similarity."

"Yes," Cherrill said.

"If you can find a point of dissimilarity, does that shake your conviction?"

"It must interfere with the identification."

Flowers nodded and turned his attention to the image of the print lifted from the mirror. With a wooden pointer, he tapped the left side of the print and began to trace the path of the looping pattern, detailing the number of ridges and brakes in the continuity of the swirls. The points of similarity between the two prints had been numbered one through twenty five. Throughout his questioning, Flowers grilled Cherrill as to every minor discrepancy between the two impressions. Why, he wanted to know, was the distance between some ridges on one print, twice that of the distance between corresponding ridges on the other print? Why, also, was one ridge on one print wider than the same ridge on the other print? Surely, such dissimilarities cast the identification of Gordon Frederick Cummins as the killer of Evelyn Oatley into some doubt.

"How can it be? If there is an enlargement of the thumb mark and an enlargement of the prisoner's thumb mark, and—if in fact—you get points of similarity which you point out—how can it be that if you follow a ridge round from one of your points to another point, on one of those marks there are four ridges, and on the other one there are five ridges? How is that possible if the same person made both marks?"

"The explanation in this case is quite simple," Cherrill said. "There was a movement of the thumb on the mirror, which has slightly distorted it. The thumb might have moved when the original impression was made, and two ridges run into one. We often meet that. It makes no difference to the identification whatsoever. In all probability, in this case, the mirror moved; it was dropped back into the handbag."

Flowers nodded. "Does that not make it extremely difficult to identify a mark either of a moving thumb or of a still thumb upon a moving object, as compared with the mark of a still thumb upon a still object?"

"I admit that—but it is not impossible," Cherrill said. "We do it every day."

Sir Bernard Spilsbury also found his integrity under fire when Flowers approached him on the witness stand. The pathologist testified that the cause of Evelyn Oatley's death had been the deep gash to her neck, which probably bled the life out of her in less than five minutes. Asked by Flowers at what time he arrived at the victim's apartment, Spilsbury said 12:30 p.m. on the afternoon of February 10. Based on rigor mortis and the woman's cooling body temperature, the austere Spilsbury told Flowers that he estimated the woman's time of death to be "approximately" 12:30 a.m.

"Are you saying definitely that this woman was dead at 12:30 a.m.?" Flowers asked.

"I said approximately," Spilsbury said. "I cannot say to the minute or to the half hour or to the hour."

Flowers raised his eyebrows in a show of theatrical curiosity. "I do not want there to be too much vagueness about it," he said. "Does that mean within a quarter of an hour of 12:30 a.m., one way or the other?"

"No," Spilsbury said, his voice flat, "one could not speak as nearly as that."

"Then within what boundary?"

"I should say within two hours either way," Spilsbury said, "either two hours before half-past twelve, or two hours after half-past twelve—but half-past twelve being the most probable time."

"So," Flowers said, "we are getting back to 10:30 p.m. on the ninth, or 2:30 a.m. on the tenth?"

"Yes."

The direction Flowers was attempting to lead Spilsbury with his questioning was clear. If the victim had indeed died at 10:30 p.m. on February 9, then it could not have been Cummins who killed her. This fact was bore out by Felix Sampson, summoned to the stand by the prosecution. The cadet testified that he went out with Cummins on the night of the killing. Questioned by McClure, Sampson detailed for the jury how he and Cummins met two prostitutes outside the Monico Restaurant in Piccadilly Circus between 10:30 p.m. and 11 p.m. Liking what they saw, the two men agreed to meet back outside the Monico Restaurant after taking care of business.

"When did you get back to the rendezvous point?"

"It was about eleven-thirty," Sampson said, testifying that he waited roughly twenty-five minutes for Cummins to return before venturing off on his own for the remainder of the evening. At six o'clock the following morning, he ascended the fire escape outside St. James's Close with all the care of a burglar and snuck into his billet through the kitchen window. Tiptoeing to his bunk, he found Cummins in bed.

"I asked him what time he got in," Sampson said. "He said about half-past three or four."

Sampson testified that Cummins told him he had not been satisfied with his original choice of woman that evening. Wanting to spend time with someone more compatible with his particular tastes, he wandered back to Piccadilly Circus. This differed from what Cummins had told Greeno during the interrogation at Brixton Prison. Called by the prosecution, Greeno read Cummins's statement in which the airman told the detective he and Sampson had rendezvoused after their respective encounters and taken a bus back to St. James's Close. The reading of the statement concluded with Cummins saying he and Sampson were so drunk, their bunkmates were forced to help them to bed.

The defense grilled Greeno on his interview tactics. John Flowers handled the questioning and sought to portray the detective as a bully who terrified Cummins into confessing. Flowers referred to Cummins's admission that he had gone off with a prostitute that night.

"I put it to you that when he said he had gone off with a woman, you thought that you had got an admission from him that he had gone off with Evelyn Oatley," Flowers said.

"I thought no such thing!" Greeno said.

"Did you not say to him, 'Now I shall get a rope around your neck,' or words to that effect?"

"Certainly not," Greeno said.

"I put it that you frightened the life out of him after he told you about going off with this woman."

"I did no such thing," Greeno said, controlling his temper, "no such thing."

Flowers sought to further portray the detective as a terror monger when he called Cummins to the stand. The young airman stood in the witness box, his hands clasped nervously in front of him. For the jurors, he put on the act of a well-to-do sort bewildered by his current circumstance.

"Would you tell My Lord and the jury what, if anything, had been said to you by Mr. Greeno just before you made that part of your statement?" Flowers asked.

Casting a quick glance in Greeno's direction, Cummins said, "Mr. Greeno told me, 'We have a rope round your neck and are going to hang you with it,' or words to that effect."

"That was after you said you had been with this woman?"

"Yes."

"Did that frighten you?" Flowers asked.

"It did," Cummins said.

"Remembering where you stand, and the oath you have taken, did you have anything to do with the murder of that unfortunate woman, Mrs. Oatley?"

"No," Cummins said. "I did not."

In its cross-examination of the defendant, the prosecution set out to portray Cummins's story as a loosely threaded fabric of lies.

"You were frightened by Mr. Greeno?" asked McClure, who grilled Cummins with an unrelenting barrage.

"Yes," Cummins said.

"Will you just tell the jury why you were frightened?"

"Quite naturally," Cummins said. "I was frightened because Mr. Greeno made that remark with reference to murder and hanging, and, well, I was very frightened. He frightened me."

McClure, who wanted Cummins to admit on the stand that he had lied in his statement, continued to push the matter: "I want you to tell the jury more about why you were frightened," he said. "Were you frightened because you told a lie?"

Cummins said he was.

"It is quite untrue you met Sampson again that night," McClure said.

"Yes."

Waving Cummins's statement for emphasis, McClure asked, "Between the time when you left the girls at Piccadilly Circus and the time you told Sampson that you got to bed, three-thirty, is there any living soul who knows what you did?"

"I saw no one else," Cummins said, shifting uncomfortably on the stand.

"The mistake you made—so you call it—was to say that you got back to Piccadilly Circus at about 10 p.m.," McClure said, again referring to the airman's statement. "That mistake was made before you were, as you say, frightened?"

"Yes," an increasingly nervous Cummins said. "I was very vague as to times. In my statement, all my times were wrong."

"I suggest to you it was not a mistake, and I will tell you why," McClure said. "You had to be in by half past ten if you went by the ordinary rules. Were you intending for one moment to get back to your billet by half past ten that night at all?"

"Yes," Cummins stammered. "Such was our intention at the beginning of the evening."

McClure was incensed. Again, he referred to Cummins's statement and began rattling off the various bars and restaurants Cummins and Sampson visited on the night in question, referencing the two men's impressive intake of alcohol. "You're telling the jury you intended to get back to your billet by ten-thirty?"

"Yes," Cummins said. "Early in the evening, that was our intent—when we had not had so much to drink."

Under McClure's cross-examination, Cummins admitted he and Sampson had not even met the two prostitutes in Piccadilly Circus until nearly eleven that night, and partially blamed the violation of his curfew on the blackout. "I had not a watch, myself," he said. "And, of course, in the dark one cannot see public clocks."

As seemingly noble as Cummins's efforts were to deflect McClure's vicious inquisition, his performance lacked sincerity. He could not account for the discrepancies between his statement and that of Sampson. It proved a simple case of a lie being so blatant there was no way to work around it. Not even another untruth could cover up his distortion of the facts. McClure brutalized Cummins with his questioning, relishing the chance to reveal the smooth airman as nothing more than a thief and murderer. Cummins could offer no explanation as to how the victim's cigarette case wound up in his billet, nor could he present the names of anyone who might be able to verify his story. Furthermore, while he insisted he had never been to a flat on Wardour Street, he could not explain away the fingerprints that were found on the tin opener and piece of broken mirror recovered from the apartment. The more Cummins tried to save his neck, the more pathetic his excuses became. When he finally conceded that certain aspects of Sampson's statement were correct, he blamed the passage of time and alcohol for blurring his recollection. This did little to advance his cause, for Sampson had drunk just as much as Cummins, who had given his original statement to police less than a week after the murder.

Cummins's attorneys could not fix the damage.

On Tuesday, April 28, both sides presented their closing arguments to the jury. Transcripts of the trial do not record what the attorneys said, but they do quote Justice Asquith's summation of the case. Elaborating for more than an hour, the judge reviewed the key points in the cases brought by the defense and prosecution. Surely, the defense had argued, the man who slaughtered Evelyn Oatley would have been drenched in blood in the immediate aftermath, yet Cummins's uniform and other clothing police retrieved bore no such stains. The prosecution simply countered by presenting evidence that the fatal cut to Evelyn Oatley's neck damaged "not an artery which spurts, but a vein which flows." The dissimilarities mentioned by the defense between the fingerprints lifted from the crime scene and those taken from Cummins were also addressed by Asquith, though the justice's recounting of the testimony lent credence to the prosecution's position.

"It must occur to you, even if it had not been pointed out, as men of common sense, that a fingerprint accidentally made will seldom, if ever, correspond to a fingerprint which is taken by Scotland Yard," Asquith told the jury. "At the Yard, the fingertip is cleaned with alcohol or petrol so as to wipe away all sweat and dirt, and it is then pressed with a pressure that is neither too excessive or gentle on a smooth, level, artificially prepared surface after having been inked. If you contrast that with a natural fingerprint made by accident, there are obvious and clear differences."

In debating the fingerprint evidence, Asquith urged the jurors to keep in mind the fact that Cherrill was "a man with a quarter of a century's experience in this matter and probably the greatest expert in the Kingdom . . . He has said that not only is he positive but he is prepared to stake his reputation that his opinion is right."

Looking at Cummins, Asquith said, "A sadistic sexual murder has been committed here of a ghoulish and horrible type, but of a type which is not at all uncommon, and that has been done by somebody. What you have to determine is whether, upon the evidence, it has been proved beyond reasonable doubt that the murderer was the man who stands in the dock. His life and liberty are in your hands, but in your hands also are the interests of society."

The jury retired to consider its verdict at 4 p.m. The deliberations lasted only thirty-five minutes. As the men filed back into the quiet courtroom, they avoided making eye contact with the defendant—a disquieting sign for Cummins's attorneys. Asked by the court clerk as to the jury's verdict upon its hasty return, the foreman replied, "Guilty of murder."

The clerk turned to face Cummins. "Prisoner at the bar," he said, "you stand convicted of murder. Have you anything to say why the court should not give you judgment of death, according to the law?"

This question was more a matter of British judicial custom than a chance to change the justice's mind. A woman could plead for clemency if she was pregnant, while a man, up until 1827, could escape the hangman's noose if he was a cleric with the church. Neither situation benefited Cummins. "I am completely innocent, sir," he said, struggling to keep his voice steady.

The court chaplain approached the judge's bench and placed upon the justice's head the dreaded black cap, a piece of black silk measuring nine inches square that was donned prior to a sentencing of death. Asquith cleared his throat and eyed the defendant. In the public gallery, Cummins's wife wept.

"Gordon Frederick Cummins," Asquith said, "after a fair trial you have been found guilty, and on a charge of murder, as you know, there is only one sentence which the law permits me to pronounce, and that is that you be taken from this place to a lawful prison, and thence to a place of execution, and that you be there hanged by the neck until you are dead. And may the Lord have mercy upon your soul."

The court chaplain, who had sat through the trial, concluded the proceeding with a forceful "Amen."

TWENTY

Judicial hangings in Britain were a morning affair, generally scheduled for eight o'clock within the London county limits, at whatever prison had been designated the place of execution. It was a highly technical process and required the most exquisite attention so as to avoid any mishaps that would further enhance the condemned's already considerable anguish. The Home Office oversaw the rules governing hangings, which were typically attended by a small gathering of witnesses. Watching the prisoner fall through the trapdoor were the prison doctor, the prison governor and two warders. The hangman would go about his job with brutal efficiency, moving the process along as quickly as he could. From the time of sentencing to the moment of execution, a minimum of three Sundays had to pass, thus ensuring all legal avenues for the prisoner had been exhausted. Tuesday was typically designated the day of execution. For Cummins, his date with the hangman fell on June 25, 1942, at Wandsworth Prison.

His final three months had been spent in a "condemned cell," a drab and squalid place of gray stone walls and floor. It afforded little in the way of comfort other than a small cot, a commode and a sink. If the condemned were lucky, he might have a bathtub. The cell was larger than most, for it was two cells knocked into one. Teams of two or three guards took turns watching the prisoner around the clock, eliminating any sense of privacy. The cell was generally no more than twenty feet from the gallows, and a wardrobe pushed against one of the walls actually concealed the door leading to the death chamber. At the last possible moment, a warder—or guard—would slide the wardrobe aside and enter the cell to take the condemned to the hangman's noose. While some prisons had permanent gallows, others did not. For the latter, the proper equipment would be sent for on the occasion from London's Pentonville Prison. The shipment would arrive by train and include all the necessary accoutrements of execution, including hood, straps and ropes. The hood was white and looked not unlike a typical pillowcase. It was pulled over the condemned's head at the last moment. This part of the process had been reached through trial and error. When the hood was placed on the prisoner while he was still in his cell, execution officials found that it only increased the terror level, for the prisoner could not see anything happening around him. If, however, the prisoner was allowed to survey his surroundings on the way to the gallows, it helped—in some strange way—to placate the nerves.

Hanging was a precise science, drawing on mathematics and extensive calculations. The weight and height of a prisoner were pivotal factors in the planning of an execution. During his final months, Cummins was weighed daily, and on the day before his execution, he was eyed carefully by the hangman, who took note of Cummins's height and weight and mentally applied it to a formula that included the length of the rope and the length of the drop. Before Cummins stood atop the trapdoor, there would be a trial run using a bag of sand that weighed approximately the same amount as the condemned. The very piece of rope that would go round Cummins's neck would be tied to the sandbag, which would be left to hang overnight to remove any stretch from the rope. If the rope stretched during the hanging, the force of the rope against the prisoner's neck would not be as great and would only increase the condemned's suffering. The rope had its own special qualities. It was thirteen feet in length and made of Italian silk hemp—smooth, but strong. It's chamois leather binding prevented chafing of the skin. By the time Cummins stepped onto the gallows, the noose had gone through some minor design changes to ensure that it killed more efficiently. Originally, nooses had been made by looping one end of rope through the other. Now the free end of the rope was fed through a brass eyelet that was carefully positioned under the angle of the left jaw. When the rope snapped tight, it was pivotal that the force of the sudden stop pass through the spine along the back of the neck, breaking it and causing near-immediate unconsciousness. If the front of the neck took the brunt of the stop, a miserable death would result from slow strangulation.

Cummins spent his final months in prison pacing back and forth, reading when he could and meeting with family. Visits were allowed, though a glass partition separated loved ones from the condemned. On the morning of the execution, the bag of sand was untied from the rope. Whatever final adjustments needed to be made to the rope and the length of the drop were made. At 7 a.m., the rope was coiled up and readied. A set of Cummins's own clothes was brought to the cell, where he changed into dark trousers and a white shirt. He was briefly examined by the prison doctor, who gave him a glass of brandy to calm the nerves. This was common practice, though tranquilizers were forbidden. Just before 8 a.m., the wardrobe against the wall of Cummins's cell slid to the side, revealing the entrance to the execution room. The hangman entered with two warders, who stood on either side of Cummins. The prisoner's hands were placed behind his back and securely fastened with a leather strap.

Without saying a word, the hangman led the way out of the cell into the execution room. Cummins followed, with the warders accompanying him by each elbow. He was led straight to the trapdoor, above which the noose hung at chest level. A large, white "T" had been drawn on the trapdoor in chalk, indicating where the prisoner was to stand. Two prison officers who stood on either side of the trap made sure Cummins was properly situated. Once Cummins was in place, the hangman pulled the white execution hood over his face. The noose was put around his neck, and his ankles were fastened with another leather strap. The noose's brass eyelet was placed below the left angle of the jaw and secured in place by a stopper. Quickly, the hangman removed a safety pin from the base of the trapdoor-release lever. With a pull of the wooden handle, the floor gave way beneath Cummins's feet. His body fell through the door into the cell below, the free length of rope uncoiling until it sprang tight and snapped Cummins's neck with an audible click. The body jerked and twisted, the legs twitched in a brief, but violent, spasm. Then Cummins was still. His body swayed gently back and forth at the end of the rope, the gallows beam above creaking with the strain of his weight. The whole process had taken little more than a minute.

The prison doctor approached the dangling form with his stethoscope at the ready. He steadied the body and listened for Cummins's heartbeat. A weak, arrhythmic beat could be heard. Each successive beat grew weaker until, several minutes later, there was nothing. The doctor nodded. The execution chamber was cleared, and Cummins was left to hang for an hour before his body was let down and carted away for the official autopsy. Custom called for prison officials to measure the deceased's neck after hanging to determine how far it had been stretched. Generally, the neck was elongated by one to two inches.

It was two prison orderlies who came to take Cummins's body away. By the time they entered the death chamber, his body had stopped swinging. It hung there, motionless, the neck bent backward at a sharp angle. They placed a stretcher on the stone floor beneath the dead man's feet. One orderly grasped Cummins by the legs as the other climbed a short stepladder to remove the noose from the neck. Somewhere, in the skies above, bombers approached. And as Cummins's body was removed from the end of the rope, the air-raid sirens in London began their mournful wail.

A NOTE ON SOURCES

The primary source material for *In the Dark* were the Scotland Yard case files now kept at the British National Archives in Kew, London. The detailed statements by witnesses and the novel-quality case review by Detective Chief Inspector Edward Greeno paint a wonderful—if not dark—picture of 1940s life and crime in London. In addition to police documents, I also consulted the trial transcripts. The level of detail in these official records is stunning. The documents are catalogued at the archives as follows:

DPP 2/989—Cummins: Murder 4 Cases. Attempted Murder 2 Cases: 1942.
DPP 2/952—Cummins: Appeal. Murder: 1942.
Crim 1/1397—Defendant: Cummins, Gordon Frederick. Charge: Murder. Sessions: April 1942.

Dialogue that appears in this book is derived from these records. Writing *In the Dark*, I consulted only a few secondary sources. For details of general life in wartime London I referred to Felicity Goodall's wonderful book, *Voices from the Home Front: Personal Experiences in Wartime Britain 1939–45* (David & Charles, 2004). *An Underworld at War: Spivs, Deserters, Racketeers and Civilians in the Second World War* by Donald Thomas

(John Murray, 2003) was a great source of information on criminal activity in 1940s London. Details on some of Scotland Yard's previous exploits, such as the case of Dr. Crippen, the "Vault of Vice" trial and the advent of the "murder bag" come from *Famous Cases of Scotland Yard's Murder Squad* by Tom Tullet (Triad/Granada, 1981). Additional details of the Yard's history were derived from the websites of London's Metropolitan Police Department and the city's central criminal court, the Old Bailey.

Details on judicial hanging procedures were found at the online resource Capital Punishment UK.

Simon Reed lives in the San Francisco Bay Area, where he works as an award-winning newspaper reporter. He is the author of two previous works of nonfiction, *On the House: The Bizarre Killing of Michael Malloy* and *The Killing Skies: RAF Bomber Command at War,* and has appeared on Court TV's "The Investigators." Although fascinated with murder, he's a pretty nice guy. You can reach him through his website, www.simonread.com

Penguin Group (USA) Online

What will you be reading tomorrow?

Tom Clancy, Patricia Cornwell, W.E.B. Griffin,
Nora Roberts, William Gibson, Robin Cook,
Brian Jacques, Catherine Coulter, Stephen King,
Dean Koontz, Ken Follett, Clive Cussler,
Eric Jerome Dickey, John Sandford,
Terry McMillan, Sue Monk Kidd, Amy Tan,
John Berendt…

You'll find them all at
penguin.com

*Read excerpts and newsletters,
find tour schedules and reading group guides,
and enter contests.*

Subscribe to Penguin Group (USA) newsletters
and get an exclusive inside look
at exciting new titles and the authors you love
long before everyone else does.

PENGUIN GROUP (USA)
us.penguingroup.com